~ TRIP ~

THE ANNUAL HOLIDAY OF GWR'S SWINDON WORKS

~ TRIP ~

THE ANNUAL HOLIDAY OF GWR'S SWINDON WORKS

ROSA MATHESON

TEMPUS

Dedicated to unsung heroes Trevor Cockbill and Jack Hayward:
champions of Swindon's railway history.

Front cover top: 'Bound for the West', County Class 4-4-0s 3832 *County of Wilts* and 3824 *County of Somerset* await the 'right of way' in 1912. They are pulled up alongside the carriage works preparing to head west to 'Swindon-by-the-Sea', Weymouth or perhaps Weston-super-Mare. Only a thin strip of wire separates the Trippers from the mainline!

Front cover bottom: Waiting at Old Town Station. A wonderfully atmospheric photo capturing the excitement of TRIP re-instated in 1946. All are smartly turned out. The flat caps have disappeared and just a few gentlemen sport trilbys. Henry 'Harry' Haines, a coppersmith in K. Shop, seen in the foreground, is taking his wife Florence, older daughter Doreen in fashionable sunglasses, and little daughter Carole wearing red jumper with white ducks, hugging her precious bucket and perched on the suitcase, off to the seaside. The platform is full to bursting and everyone is smiling and full of happy anticipation.

Back cover: Trippers at Tenby Station with their luggage aboard handcarts to be conveyed from to their lodgings. Notice the two gentlemen Trippers already in smart new daps.

First published 2006

Tempus Publishing Limited
The Mill, Brimscombe Port,
Stroud, Gloucestershire, GL5 2QG
www.tempus-publishing.com

© Rosa Matheson, 2006

The right of Rosa Matheson to be identified as the Author
of this work has been asserted in accordance with the
Copyrights, Designs and Patents Act 1988.

British Library Cataloguing in Publication Data.
A catalogue record for this book is available from the British Library.

ISBN 0 7524 3909 X

Typesetting and origination by Tempus Publishing Limited.
Printed in Great Britain.

CONTENTS

Trevor Cockbill, whose father had a passion for St Ives, poses nonchalantly by its seafront. Trevor was interested in Swindon's railway heritage and wrote several books about Swindon and the Mechanics Institution.

Jack Hayward relaxes in the garden of his cottage in the railway village. Jack worked as a clerk 'Inside' in various shops and offices. A self-taught historian, Jack is passionate about the recording and preservation of Swindon's railway history. He has contributed a number of articles to the *North Star* magazine. Jack assisted me in the research for my doctorate thesis on women in the Works and also for TRIP.

ACKNOWLEDGEMENTS

This book could not have been achieved without the interest and support of the many people who have shown kindness and generosity of spirit to an overwhelming degree. An enormous vote of thanks is owed to all. My list is long, but should I have inadvertently overlooked anyone, I humbly apologise whilst offering my thanks. For anyone whose photographs/postcards are reproduced and I have been unable to trace, it is hoped this sincere acknowledgement is accepted.

To all those who shared their family histories, TRIP memories and photos with me: Mrs Jean Allen, Councillor Derek Benfield, Mr John Cheesley, Mr Ronald Clack, Mrs Millicent Cox, Mr Cyril Cox, Mrs Kath Bridges, Miss Lorna Dawes, Mr John 'Jack' Fleetwood, Mr Charlie Gee, Mr Ron Glass, Mr Ivor Jenkins, Mrs Ivy Lawrence, Captain Philip Moran, Mrs Joyce Murgatroyd, Mr Peter Pragnall, Mrs Diane Shaw *née* Turner, Mrs Jean Spicer *née* Dickson, Mrs Mary Sturley *née* Ruddick, Mr Frank Saunders, Mrs Stella Taylor, Mrs Margaret Suffolk *née* Long, Mr John Walsh, Mrs Jan Ward.

To others, for different kinds of help: Jack Hayward for all his research, archives, photos, general assistance and keeping me going; Revd Brian Arman for his brainstorming sessions, help with captions, use of photos and printed material; Ken Gibbs for his drawing and experiences; Eddie Lyons for his specialist knowledge; Tom Richards; John Mudge; Brian Cockbill for use of their printed work; Dave Ellis; Ken Tanner and the members of the Thursday morning Ex-Railway Workers Club, for sharing their memories and knowledge; Norman Wakely and Dave Ellis for their knowledge of TRIP working; Jack Willcock for his editorial reading and use of his railway library; Ken Daniels for his interest, knowledge and use of photos of Tenby; Peter Gray, Derek Frost, Roy Nash and David Bedford for use of photos, information and postcards; Neil Lover for help with the cover photograph; STEAM, Museum of the Great Western Railway, for help and use of materials; Swindon Museum and Art Gallery; Roger Trayhern and the team at SBC Reference Library; Maureen Atwell for local knowledge and source material on Weymouth; the Weymouth Reference Library team; the Public Record Office, Kew; Ian Allan Publishing for allowing me to quote from their publication *The Day of the Holiday Express: Western Region Services on 9 July 1960;* The *Tenby Times*, The *Southern Times*, The *Evening Advertiser*; The St Ives Trust; Swindonweb for giving me a webpage to ask for help; Mrs Valerie Hillary and Mrs Margaret Suffolk for use of their poems.

Last, but definitely not least, thanks to my husband Ian, for all the care, cups of tea and dinners made whilst I worked, and my family – James, Hanna-Gael, Iainthe and Oona – for their interest and support.

INTRODUCTION

Trip: such a funny little word. What does it mean? It can have so many meanings. Trip – to fall over. Trip – to work a mechanism. Trip – to skip or dance lightly. Trip – to go on a journey. But TRIP, if you happened to be a Swindonian and one who worked 'Inside,' was *the* event of the year. Mention the word 'TRIP' in Swindon, even nowadays, and especially to someone who themselves or whose relatives worked 'Inside' the famous Great Western Railway's Swindon Works and a special, vague look comes into their eyes, a smile hangs around the edges of their mouths and a knowing shake of the head accompanies the words, 'Oh, TRIP, now that *was* really something', and what a thing it was. TRIP was an event unique to Swindon; although it related only to the employees of the Great Western Railway Co. (the GWR) and their families, who were members of the Mechanics' Institution and later employees and their families of British Railways Western Region (BR/WR), such was its impact that it affected all the inhabitants of Swindon as well as many other towns and stations up and down the Great Western line. Over the years the tradition of TRIP became part of the fabric of life for the railwaymen of Swindon Works and their families. They invested it with their own individual rituals and meanings alongside those of the community and company. They used the word TRIP like others use 'Christmas' or 'Easter'. 'Where're you going TRIP?' was the question on everyone's lips once Christmas was over. TRIP was something that was talked about with hushed breath and hopeful longing for many months before the event and is now remembered long years after with great fondness, tinged with respect and awe. It is a respect that is well earned as TRIP was an awesome project requiring mammoth planning and meticulous attention to detail – otherwise some poor bloke and his family was likely to be left behind waiting desolately at an empty sidings or station!

So what was this thing called TRIP and how did it become the stuff that myths and legends are made off? How did it develop into what O.S. Nock called, 'the most extensive, complex and highly organised movement of railway excursionists that this country has ever seen?' and what made it 'the most moving of simple human dramas in the world'? Well...

Opposite above: A large group of elegantly clad Edwardian Trippers pose for the TRIP photo. The trees in the background locate this train standing alongside St Mark's churchyard. Being railway people they would have been aware of the danger posed by the main down line seen here in the foreground. The photographer would have taken his life in his hands, however positioned, as he must be, between the down and up lines.

Opposite below: 1934 and another TRIP Special stands in the same place and another generation of Trippers pose for the camera. The styles of clothes have changed but still the Trippers dress up in their best to travel to their TRIP destinations. First in the line on the right side is young Cyril Cox in his smart knickerbockers suit reserved for Chapel and TRIP.

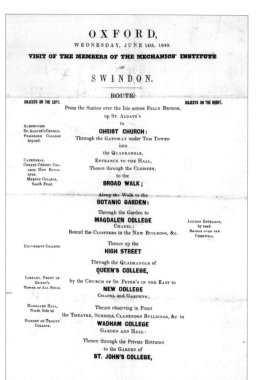

OXFORD,

WEDNESDAY, JUNE 14th, 1848.

VISIT OF THE MEMBERS OF THE MECHANICS' INSTITUTE

OF

S W I N D O N.

ROUTE:

OBJECTS ON THE LEFT.		OBJECTS ON THE RIGHT.
	From the Station over the Isis across FOLLY BRIDGE, up ST. ALDATE'S	
	to	
ALMSHOUSES. ST. ALDATE'S CHURCH. PEMBROKE COLLEGE beyond.	**CHRIST CHURCH:** Through the GATEWAY under TOM TOWER into the QUADRANGLE,	
CATHEDRAL. CORPUS CHRISTI COLLEGE NEW BUILDINGS, 1806. MERTON COLLEGE, South Front.	ENTRANCE TO THE HALL, Thence through the CLOISTER, to the **BROAD WALK;**	
	Along the Walk to the **BOTANIC GARDEN:**	
	Through the Garden to **MAGDALEN COLLEGE** CHAPEL: Round the Cloisters to the New Building, &c.	LONDON ENTRANCE, by road. BRIDGE OVER THE CHERWELL.
UNIVERSITY COLLEGE.	Thence up the **HIGH STREET**	
LIBRARY, FRONT OF QUEEN'S. TOWER OF ALL SOULS.	Through the Quadrangle of **QUEEN'S COLLEGE,** by the CHURCH of ST. PETER'S IN THE EAST to **NEW COLLEGE** Chapel and Gardens;	
MAGDALEN HALL, North Side of. GARDEN OF TRINITY COLLEGE.	Thence observing in Front the Theatre, Schools, Clarendon Buildings, &c. to **WADHAM COLLEGE** GARDEN and HALL:	
	Thence through the Private Entrance to the GARDEN of **ST. JOHN'S COLLEGE,**	

The itinerary of the very first TRIP, a visit to Oxford shows what a splendid event it was, planned down to the very last detail. This set the standard for future TRIP planning and organisation.

OBJECTS ON THE LEFT.		OBJECTS ON THE RIGHT.
	Through the College to ST. GILES'S STREET, to the **MARTYRS' MEMORIAL, ST. MARY MAGDALEN CHURCH;**	TAYLOR BUILDINGS, UNIVERSITY GALLERIES. WORCESTER COLLEGE, at end of Beaumont Street.
TRINITY COLLEGE.	Thence up BROAD STREET passing the Front of BALLIOL COLLEGE, the New Buildings of EXETER, the Ashmolean Museum, the Theatre;	TUAL STREET, containing, EXETER, JESUS, AND LINCOLN COLLEGES.
	Then up the steps of the **CLARENDON BUILDINGS** to the **THEATRE,** then through the **DIVINITY SCHOOLS** into the Schools' Quadrangle: to the **BODLEIAN LIBRARY AND GALLERY,** thence to the	
MAGDALEN HALL. ALL SOULS' COLLEGE.	**RADCLIFFE LIBRARY,** and thence, through the side entrance, to **ALL SOULS' COLLEGE LIBRARY,**	BRASENOSE COLLEGE.
ORIEL STREET, leading to ST. MARY HALL, ORIEL COLLEGE, &c.	Thence through the College up the HIGH STREET to the **TOWN HALL.**	ST. MARY'S CHURCH. ALL SAINTS' CHURCH. ST. MARTIN'S CHURCH, OR CARFAX.

IN THE AFTERNOON

The following places may be visited in parties (not exceeding thirty individuals) on production of the Company's Tickets:

THE NEW UNIVERSITY GALLERIES, ASHMOLEAN MUSEUM, GEOLOGICAL MUSEUM, AND APPARATUS FOR LECTURES IN EXPERIMENTAL PHILOSOPHY, in the CLARENDON BUILDINGS. ROOF OF THE RADCLIFFE LIBRARY, and view from thence, And the College Gardens. } Before 5 P.M.

Already TRIP Pass has taken on significance as it is only by showing the 'Company's Ticket' that the Trippers can attend the afternoon tours. It would appear that the hosts have not realised that the tickets were, in fact, issued by The Institute.

— CHAPTER 1 —

HOW IT ALL BEGAN

The origins of TRIP lay in the birth of New Swindon and the fortunes of the Great Western Railway Co. With the development of the GWR's Bristol to London line it became necessary to find an appropriate site for stabling the variety of engines necessary for tackling the various gradients and difficulties encountered along the route in different directions. Upon the recommendation of Daniel Gooch, the company's new locomotive superintendent who had so impressed Brunel despite his young age that he had been happily offered the post, it was decided that the green fields below Swindon were the best site for the proposed principle engine establishment of the company and that a station at Swindon would be generally very helpful, and so was born New Swindon.

In his diary Daniel Gooch records that the machinery at what was to become known worldwide as 'Swindon Works' was set to work on 28 November 1842 and that the factory began work on 2 January 1943.[1] Skilled men were needed to run the Works, operate the machinery and to service the engines stabled there. As there was no local heavy industry to recruit from, men with such skills had to be brought in from afar. They came from northern England, from Bristol, Scotland and London to this new frontier-town. The first batch of the company cottages to house these employees just opposite the Works were quickly built and as quickly filled with the workmen and their families; there were often two or sometimes, in desperate times, three families to a cottage, plus the odd handful of lodgers! By January 1847, 1,360 persons were being accommodated in 182 completed village houses with yet a further 978 people living in the area immediately outside the village. The village was, according to the young diarist Edward Snell who lived there at the time, 'a precious place', with 'not a knocker or scraper in the whole place'. It was a damp, muddy and an extremely expensive place to live as, 'the Company make the men pay most extortionate rents for these bits of huts'.[2] Home comforts, shops, and entertainments were sadly lacking and the men found their relaxation in drink, so much so that their drunken revels were the reason for numerous complaints by the neighbouring gentry! Something had to be done and, according to Gooch, it was upon his suggestion that, 'workmen whose moral character was superior to their fellows... formed... into a Workmen's Institute.'[3] It may well be that the actual formation was something much less formal with 'a few kind friends'[4] getting together and circulating books amongst themselves. However or whatever the actual beginnings were, what is definitely known is that in January 1844 the New Swindon Mechanics' Institution was formally constituted and by the end of the year the membership had reached 129. Members were encouraged to meet, read, study and entertain each other together in a room within the Works.

Eventually, as membership grew, there was a need for a properly established centre and on 24 May 1854 a ceremony was held to mark the laying of the foundation stone of the the 'Mechanics' building. TRIP and the Mechanics' Institution are linked as by an umbilical cord.

In the picture can be seen three of the 'Company 'ouses' in Bathhampton Street, which was one of the earliest streets to be built, being completed in 1842 to Brunel's design. It was from these and others like them that the railway workers and their families would pour out on TRIP morning. (1968 Jack Hayward)

Every row of houses had its 'backsies', where the children would play out. In the picture we can see the roofs of the outside 'privvies' and the chimneys from coppers where they would do the washing. This 'backsie' is between Exeter and Bathampton Street looking west towards the park. The solitary figure walking down the backway would be one of hundreds on TRIP morning. (1968 Jack Hayward)

The Mechanics' Institute was made possible by the actions of Members of the Mechanics' Institution forming the New Swindon Company which raised money to enable the building to be undertaken. Completed in 1855 it provided a wide range of services for the members and was the heart of the railway community. This is where the administration of TRIP was originally undertaken by the Council members of the Institution until taken over by the Staff Office. (Jack Hayward)

The latter gave birth to the former, which grew to become an 'institution' in its own right. A local historian and Mechanics' Institution expert, Trevor Cockbill has written that the 'Mechanics' Institute earned its place in social history as a pioneer of holidays for working people.'[5]

For many years it has been debated whether TRIP actually originated in 1848 or 1849. From 1906, numerous articles in the GWR's own magazine led the way in the theory that it was 1849 with the apparent lack of any concrete evidence to establish an exact date. Many articles appeared that affirmed this supposed date. The confusion may have been caused back in 1906 by A.J.L. White when writing a small article entitled 'Swindon Workmen's Annual Trip' in the Great Western Railway's own journal. Under the heading of 'Departmental Doings', he informs his readers how he was 'afforded the opportunity, when looking up the origins of this annual excursion, of perusing the reports of the Mechanics Instututution by the courtesy of the Secretary of the Institution.' He found, he said, an extract of a report that stated:

> The Council feel that you will look back with great pleasure to your visit to Oxford in June last; on which occasion the Directors kindly granted us a special train for the conveyance of the members of the Institution to that eminent university. Each member was permitted to take a lady and in all the numbers amounted to about 500. Daniel Gooch. President.

... and surmised that this related to 1849. He was wrong.

Swindon Works railwaymen's TRIP had its origins in the illustrious city of Oxford when in June 1847 the distinguished gentlemen of the British Association for the Advancement of Science held their seventeenth session. They came together to discuss and debate the latest scientific

GREAT WESTERN RAILWAY. No.359

NEW SWINDON MECHANICS' INSTITUTION TRIP.

This Ticket is not transferable nor available in 1st Class Carriages.

Institution No. *1367*.

ON PRODUCTION OF THIS TICKET, THE BEARER,

Mr *Hawkins*, Wife, and _____ Children,

are to be allowed to travel by the *Institution Train* to **NEWTON ABBOT**,
on Friday, July 10th, 1903, returning to Swindon in Third Class Carriages,
on any day up to Friday, July 17th, 1903, as announced in separate notice
issued.

N.B.—*This Ticket will be available for the above dates* ONLY, *and care must be taken
of it, as another will not on any account be given.*

Terms and Conditions upon which this Ticket is issued.

This Ticket is issued by the Great Western Railway Company on the sole conditions that they
are not to be held liable for any pecuniary or other responsibility to the holder, or his repre-
sentatives, for loss of life or personal injury, or for delay, or loss of or damage to property
belonging to him or her that may be sustained by such person whilst using this Ticket; and its
acceptance and use shall be taken as evidence of an agreement between the holder and the
Company that the journey for which this Ticket is issued is undertaken at his or her entire risk,
and that the Company are absolved from all responsibility as aforesaid.

TRIP free pass was only available to Institute members. It bore the member's name and individual Institution number, hence, Mr Hawkins, No.1367. In the beginning these were printed and issued by the Institute. It is interesting to see that the TRIP Special Train is identified as 'the Institution train' and that the ticket can only be used in a third-class carriage. (STEAM Museum of the Great Western Railway)

attainments. These learned gentlemen were fascinated by all things scientific, philosophical or technical, and so gladly accepted an invitation and a free train provided by the Great Western Railway Co. to visit the company's workshops at Swindon, where technological inventions and advancement were the order of the day. Such was the success of the visit and such the hospitality shown to these honoured visitors that the Oxford members of the British Association felt duty bound to return the compliment.

A small article headed 'Railway Excursion' in Jackson's 'Oxford Journal', a weekly local journal, dated 10 June 1848, clears away any confusion and provides us with the actual date and details. It announces to the people of Oxford:

On Wednesday next we are to be visited by at least 500 men from the Great Western Railway Company's works at Swindon, who are to be provided with a good dinner at the expense of the University as some acknowledgement on the part of that body, of the liberality and attention shown by the company to the members of the British Association who it will be remembered, were conveyed to Swindon last summer to see the Company's works in a special train provided gratuitously by the Company.

A copy of the itinerary gives exact details of the date Wednesday 14 June 1848, as well as the content of the day.[6]

The following week, 17 June 1848, the journal was extremely happy to report on the great success that the visit had been. It tells how 'a cheerful looking cargo of upwards of 500 respectably dressed men, women and children' arrived at 8.30 a.m., off a broad-gauge train consisting of nine carriages. By prior arrangement the group was divided up into 'sections', each with its own 'leader', including three gentlemen who were members of the Oxford branch of the British Association, Revd R. Walker of Wadham, Dr Acland and Revd E. Hill of Christ Church, along with members of the university. The party was escorted up and down, in and out the breadth and width of the colleges and other notable places of interest. They were then conducted to the Town Hall where a 'substantial cold dinner' had been prepared and 'tastefully laid-out... on five tables extending the whole length of the Hall'. Here, every effort was made by their hosts to 'promote the comfort of the people'. Short, but appropriate addresses were made and there was much hearty cheering by the visitors for the BA, for the queen, the university, the Mayor and then the queen again. Finally, the National Anthem was sung to round this part of things off. After that there was more to visit and a time for leisurely meanderings, until at 7 p.m. they were called together by the playing of a brass band, formed from members of the Institute. All then 'went in procession to the station and were soon seated on the train, which steamed away, amidst great cheering and waving of hats and handkerchiefs'. The article finished in no doubt that there would be 'pleasant recollections on both sides' as 'everything {had} passed off as orderly and as satisfactorily as could have possibly have been desired.' On that day a mould had been made and the benchmark set, and so from 1848 until the middle of the 1970s, TRIP would be a masterpiece of planning, preparation, delivery and satisfactory outcomes.

The wonder of TRIP was that the train journey was free, courtesy of the directors of the GWR, for the men and their school-age families. This was a touch of luxury for the generally low-paid railway workers who would not otherwise have been able to take their families away by train. The luxury of a free pass for TRIP was not, however, available to all the men engaged at the works – it was something that came through membership of the Mechanics' Institution. Not all men were members of the Institution, some by choice, some possibly not being able to afford it, and some because they had not worked sufficient time to become eligible for membership. An article in the *Swindon Advertiser* in 1870 informs that five trains were required for Trippers this year and that, 'the privilege of travelling on them being confined to such members of the Mechanics Institute who have paid up their subscriptions'. Decades later, Alfred Williams, a self-educated man who worked as a hammerman in Swindon Works in the early 1900s, confirms that this is still the case. He wrote of his experiences working for the GWR in his book *Life in a Railway Factory,* and writes informatively and descriptively about TRIP. He says:

> The privilege of travelling free by the TRIP Trains is not granted to all workmen, but only those who are members of the local Railway Institute and Library and have contributed about six shillings per annum to the general fund.[7].

Indeed, anyone found to be travelling on a TRIP pass who should not have been put their livelihood in jeopardy, as one unfortunate man found out. A works' notice dated 20 June 1856 and signed by the then Works' Manager and vice-president of the Institute, Minard C. Rea, states:

> I have discharged Timothy Hartley, Erector, from the Company service for having travelled by the Institution Excursion train on Saturday last with a pass that did not belong to him; and if I could discover the party who transferred to Hartley the pass he used on this occasion, that person also should be dismissed from the Service.

Eventually, after nationalisation, all employees in Swindon Works became eligible to travel free on TRIP Special Trains as part of the free 'annual pass' system. These annual passes applied across the workforce. They would often be negotiated in lieu of wage increases, and what class of pass you had and how many you received, depended on what level of grade you had. Previous Institutution members, however, still retained their extra free 'Institute Pass' to use on TRIP. The other amazing element of TRIP, and what made it distinctive from other 'Wake Weeks' or Company Excursions, was that it was not confined to one destination. Everyone could go where they liked. Initially this was confined to anywhere on the GWR system, but in a very short time it could be anywhere in the country, or even abroad. Also, after a very short period of time, not everyone had to travel on the same day, or come back on the same day. You just had to make up your mind beforehand and stick to it afterwards.

The mammoth task of TRIP was organised by the Council of Mechanics' Institution in co-operation with the Locomotive, Carriage & Wagon Committee and later the Staff Office. The bulk of the Council's work fell on the shoulders of the incumbent secretary. Between 1890 and 1923 this was Mr H.J. Southwell. He was recognised to be 'hard working and courteous', and, undoubtedly, he would have needed to be during the many years he oversaw the excursion.

The Institute would order and pay for the printing of TRIP special tickets. The cost for this was recorded in the Institution's Annual Report. Between 1884 and 1890 it came under the heading of 'Management' and between 1907 and 1914 under the heading 'Sundries.' It was always a significant amount.

Management		Sundries	
1884	£13	1890	£17 11s 1d
1885	£14	1907	£83 14 s 8d
1886	£15 0s 7d	1909	£80 17s 4d
1889	£16 15s 0d	1910	£71 01s 0d
		1911	£91 01s 6d
		1912	£75 10s 4d
		1913	£85 17s 2d
		1914	£94 02s 11d

The Council would organise the procedure of application for the tickets. Forms had to be distributed out to the hundreds, and later thousands, of men. These were filled in and returned. Each ticket then had to have the member's name handwritten on and be signed by an authorised officer of the Institute. The tickets were distributed to the men along with details of their train, times and journey, should they need to change on the way. This was just one aspect of the TRIP organisation. There were many others and they became more numerous and complex as TRIP grew in size and scope. Chapter 5 gives an insight into what a mammoth operation it became.

TRIP grew, both in numbers of Trippers and days of holiday. Over a decade after its initial excursion, the day's outing had grown to a three-day break, the Works closing at 6 p.m. on the Friday night until 9 a.m. on the following Tuesday. Ten years later in 1869, and thereafter, it closed at lunchtime at 1 p.m. and the men would start back to work on the following Thursday at 9 a.m. Between 1869 and 1874 it grew again. An article in the *Swindon Advertiser* in July 1870 informed its readers, 'these Annual Trips have continued for 22 successive years. The second Trip was to Torquay… for several years 1 train was sufficient, [however] this year 5 trains each accommodating over 1,000 persons [were necessary]'..

By 1874 the holiday had grown to a full nine-day break. Notice of TRIP holiday for that year states that the Works would close from '5.30pm Friday July 2nd and will be reopened at 9.0 am on Monday July 12th". In 1877 the day of closing had changed again back to the Thursday and the Works was closed from Thursday 5 July until 6 a.m. Monday 15 July, still a full nine days. During the very early period there seems to have been no set time when TRIP was taken, only that it happened sometime during the months of June and July. However, by the 1870s it had settled to regularly occuring during the early part of July. The first Friday of the month became TRIP day and that time became established as TRIP time, much to the delight of Swindon's schoolchildren. These lucky youngsters got longer summer holidays than others in Wiltshire and the rest of the country. The lucky landladies that hosted the Trippers would also have been pleased as they got an earlier start to their summer season, helping to boost their coffers.

In 1892 it was claimed that Swindon Works was, 'the largest establishment in the world for the manufacture and repair of engines, carriages and wagons, with around 10,000 men being employed under one roof.'[8] The population of New Swindon was 27,295. The number going away on TRIP that year is given as 18,248. Almost two thirds of the town departed. In 1900 the GWR magazine declared it was a record TRIP with 22,500 going away, but it was a record that was to be broken again and again. TRIP continued to grow and in its heyday in the 1920s and '30s the numbers were constantly in the mid-20,000s and over. TRIP 'peaked' in 1924 when a staggering 29,000 were despatched in thirty-one huge trains totalling 520 coaches. The numbers are breathtaking, the mechanics of the enterprise mind blowing and the management awesome. It was, undoubtedly, an excursion of extraordinary proportions – a world record-breaking achievement.

Waiting for TRIP Special for Birkenhead, departing at 6 a.m. It stands in front of early carriage works, built around 1871–75 by Armstrong to accommodate coach trimmers and finishers and new women workers. In the background we can see the Water Tower (c.1871) in Bristol Street which supplied water to the sawmills and incorporated the first sprinkler system in the Works, and also the tall spire of St Mark's church, built for the railway congregation. Casual Trippers wander between the Bristol line and the Gloucester line, waiting for the off.

This picure from around 1912, captures the anticipation of setting off on an exciting journey. Some Trippers have clearly made an early claim for seats, whilst others wait patiently to board. This stock, built around 1876–80, will already have done years of good service for TRIP.

HOLIDAY HUMOR.

HOLIDAYS AND AFTER

A BIT OF ALL RIGHT THIS IS

GRAND MARCH PAST   STONEY BROKE   PLEASE SIR MOTHER'S OUT   COLLECTOR

The Grand March Past, when men walked past the Pay Tables after TRIP but received no pay, has become part of the TRIP legend and was iconised in one of a series of TRIP cartoon postcards. This situation continued for almost 100 years until the Holiday with Pay Act in 1938 ensured paid leave for workers.

Regents Street was Swindon town's main shopping centre. It was, as can be seen in the picture, a very busy place except, that is, during TRIP time, when it became like the *Mary Celeste*.

Whilst undoubtedly TRIP was a great and wonderful thing and everyone speaks and writes about it in glowing terms, it must be remembered that, although the rail travel was free to members of the Institution initially, nobody received any pay for the days they were not at work. It was unpaid holiday or, seen from a different perspective, a lock-out whilst the company carried out essential maintenance and repairs.

It must have been a tough time for those on low incomes, especially those with large families. Many of them would not have been able to afford to go away and they would have had to cope at home with no money coming in and fewer shops open as the town's traders would take the opportunity to close up for their own holidays whilst such a large proportion of the town was away. The stay-at-home men could not even go off to find stop-gap work as the company was very explicit that their workmen should have only one job and being found moonlighting could cost you it. In the twentieth century, when things were more relaxed, men would go off to work on local farms, or use their skills for fellow workers.

Not everyone could go away for the whole of TRIP, even if they belonged to railway families who did. There were those who could not afford it and those whose employment kept them in town, e.g. shop girls. These would have to make do with a day away, usually mid-week, and Special TRIP Trains with reduced excursion fares for non-railway residents, would be laid on for this. TRIP Wednesday became part of TRIP tradition, Frank Saunders remembers that for these day Trippers, this was just as exciting.

And then those of us who couldn't go for the week would come down on the Wednesday... Trip Wednesday. Yeah all the shops in Town would close like... they used to close Wednesday afternoons anyway but they would close all day so that the girls could go down and see their Mam and Dad. It were good fun coming back too 'cos everybody who didn't go would turn up to greet you back. I remember my big brother coming and lifting me on his shoulders. Oh yeah, Trip was a good thing.

Jean Allen, who although coming from a railway family never managed to go away on TRIP after she started work at the age of fourteen, also remembers TRIP Wednesday:

Wednesday was the town's early closing day (still in force in the '60s and '70s) with most shops closing at 1 p.m. every week, but the first Wednesday of 'Trip' week, it was closed the whole day and many of the remaining residents, especially shop staff, took a day trip. Unwary visitors to the town on that day would complain that they couldn't even get a cup of tea. Some small

A rather wet miserable scene of Regent Street, still the town's main shopping centre with Stead & Simpson offering BARGAINS FOR TRIP. These would have included canvas shoes, sandals and most definitely 'daps'.

shops also took the opportunity to close for the week especially those in areas where most of their customers were railway workers. Those that remained open cut down on perishable stock so fresh food was a bit short for those left behind.

Mrs Jean Lockey remembers her mum saying that many shops would drop their prices during TRIP week. With so many away and the Works closed down, Swindon felt deserted, abandoned even. Dr Barbara Carter remembers it well. Her father was in charge of Accounts and so had to stay and hold the fort.

I remember as a child living in Swindon during Trip holiday… there was no one about. Everything was shut down. You couldn't buy a loaf of bread, you couldn't get anything. For that week you had to get all your stuff into the house beforehand and of course in those days we didn't have fridges. You just had to get enough to keep you going for the week. I remember I had no friends or anyone to play with. It was horrible. It was an absolute Marie Celeste of a town. Yes, it really was!

Whilst the Works was closed the management used the time to carry out essential maintenance and repair work, and specific men were held back to do this. This became known as TRIP working. John Walters' father was a foreman in L2 Shop and he invariably worked the TRIP period on the maintenance of items of plant throughout the Works. When John joined as an apprentice, he, too, stayed behind in order that he could have the same holiday as his dad. For John, TRIP working was exciting stuff.

The variety of work carried out during Trip was, to me, a 'one-off' not only because of the tasks allocated, but because the majority was without direct supervision. One year Albert Moss and myself had to change some suspect gearing in a wheel lathe in the AW Shop. The stripping down of the head and the removal of the large gearing was no small task, with the use of the walking crane for the heavy bits etc., probably just another job to the fitter, but to a couple of seventeen-year-old lads on their own – heaven.

Peter Pragnall also remembers an exciting time on TRIP working, but for quite another reason. After the factory's conversion from coal-fired steam power to oil-fired hydraulic power, the 'D' Shop gang were put on notice to dismantle the now defunct eight central coal-fired boilers and their chimneys during TRIP time. The job required extensive use of oxyacetylene torches to assist in cutting the heads off bolts. Unbeknown to D Shop gang, a fire had taken hold beneath the floorboards which then flared up during their lunch break, setting the place alight. Imagine their surprise on returning from lunch to find that they had a merry little blaze on their hands which had to be dealt with by the Works' fire brigade! Undoubtedly, TRIP was exciting for a number of different reasons and in a number of different ways!

Whilst we have looked at the facts regarding the hows and whys of TRIP, we must recognise that TRIP was about a lot more than that. For those who worked 'Inside', Christmas and TRIP were the highlights of the year. They formed the bookends of the social calendar, and the 'countdown calendar'. On returning to work after the Christmas break, men would start a countdown tally of the days to TRIP written up in chalk on their forges, the steam hammers, the factory doors, anywhere and everywhere, to remind them of what they had to look forward to and were saving hard for. Incidentally, working 'Inside' did not mean being detained at Her Majesty's pleasure, but working inside Swindon Works which was mostly contained within a large wall, so the men went literally 'Inside' to work.

Alfred Williams wrote that, 'Trip Day is the most important day in the calendar of the railway town'. It was an important day for lots of different reasons. It was important for Swindon. Swindon changed its ways and adapted itself to accommodate TRIP, so significant was it for the town's economy and social wellbeing. The council called special meetings, the shopkeepers changed their half-day closing, the local paper even closed its offices and did not print an edition on TRIP day,[9] the schools started summer holidays early, local employers adapted their holiday arrangements in keeping with TRIP. The impact on the town was huge. It visibly emptied and was left like a ghost town when the Trippers had departed. Even the factory hooter that controlled the working lives of the railway men and women, calling them to work, announcing the beginning and end of their 'dinner' break, and marking the end of the working day, and by which all Swindonians would set their clocks and watches, was stopped during TRIP, making the town feel eerily silent. TRIP was also important because of the feelings and sentiments attached to it. It was important because of the people who invested in it their feelings of hopeful anticipation and incredible excitement. Such excitement is admirably portrayed in an article in the GWR magazine about TRIP for 1903:

To the majority of peace loving citizens who appreciate the luxury of rest and the due observance of the hours of righteous slumber, it is almost an unheard of piece of eccentricity for 23,000 men, women and children to be bustling through the streets at three o'clock in the morning, edging one another aside and exhibiting a species of restless excitement born of the holiday fever.

Trippers pour out of Swindon Junction Station on their return, broke, even bankrupt, as the man says, but having had a great time and already looking forward to next year. (Swindon Museum & Art Gallery)

Scarcely had the first streak of light heralded the dawn of another day than excited persons seized with the holiday fever were moving about hither and thither, impatient that the time should seem to move along so slowly.

TRIP was about going somewhere very special – as one lady said, 'far away, the back of beyond' – and about being part of something extraordinary, where everyone who partook felt they belonged to one big railway family.

The story of TRIP is about the Great Western Railway Co., the Mechanics Institution, the gargantuan administrative organisation, the trains, the seaside destinations and Swindon's railway people. TRIP grew so that it became bigger than the sum of its parts, and became a legend in its own right.

1 Cockbill, T., *Finest Thing Out*, p15
2 Catell, p63
3 Pratt, A. , *The Life and Times of Daniel Gooch*, pp75/76
4 Cockbill, T., p20
5 Cockbill, T., p135

6 PRO Ref. RAIL 276/22
7 Williams, A., *Life in a Railway Factory*
8 'The Great Western Railway's Swindon Works 1892' Wiltshire Pamphlets No.27, SBC Library
9 *The Evening Swindon Advertiser*, 6 July 1906

━ CHAPTER TWO ━

RITUALS AND TRADITIONS

The story of TRIP has taken on an almost mythical quality, not surprisingly as TRIP played a large part in peoples' lives over many decades. When they were not actually doing it, they were planning and saving for it. As soon as Christmas was done and dusted, TRIP was the next exciting thing on the horizon. Undoubtedly, for all those who went on TRIP it was a fairy-tale[1] holiday which took them to 'another world' and made them feel like 'very special people'. TRIP *was* special, if only for all the special preparations that had to be made and put in place.

Every family had its own rituals that they liked to go through every year. Many of these were commonly shared. It is these special rituals, shared and yet individual to all families, that gave TRIP its special patterns and rhythms that added to its magical nature and brought the fairy story to life. Writing of TRIP day in 1938 when he was then a lad of twelve, Ken Ausden captures that magic when he says, 'Same routine every year. And I never got tired of it. I wish it could have gone on forever.' These routines were handed down through generations of families. Trevor Cockbill explains some of these as only someone who has lived them can. Trevor remembered:

> Every single one of us whose father worked for the GWR… looked forward to 'Trip'. It came round regularly each year, like Christmas. At home a 'mystery' was maintained as most of us did not know where our parents planned to take us in July and we knew better than to ask. A few weeks before the great event the guessing game began. Our parents played a slightly different game and warned continually that unless behaviour showed a sudden marked improvement, we would be left behind, locked in the coal house with a loaf of dry bread and a jug full of weak barley water while the rest of the family baked on Cornish beaches, or paddled in the Bristol Channel.

No one wanted to miss TRIP and everyone did their utmost to make it happen. One of the hardest rituals involved in making TRIP happen was the saving up – not a subject to be taken lightly, especially in the early days when no work meant no pay. Alfred Williams wrote feelingly about the hardships this holiday arrangement could cause:

> For several months preceding it, fathers and mothers of families, young unmarried men, and juveniles have been saving up for the outing… no part of the holiday is free, but is counted as lost time. The prompt commencement of work after Trip is, therefore, highly necessary; the great majority of the workforce are reduced to a state of absolute penury. If they have been away and spent all their money- and perhaps incurred debt at home for the rent and provisions beforehand in order to enjoy themselves the better on their trip – it will take them a considerable time to get square again.

After TRIP, money was tight as there was no pay due. 'We're not in' or 'Mam says she's out' was a very real situation for TRIP families pre-1938, when TRIP was workdays lost, or an unpaid 'lockout'.

Dressed for TRIP in their absolute best, with beautifully decorated bonnets and straw-brimmers, they are a splendid sight. How wonderfully elegant these Edwardian railway people were.

At the end of the first week after the Trip holiday there will be no money to draw. When Friday comes around bringing with it the usual hour for receiving wages, the men file out of the sheds with long faces. This is generally known in the Works as 'The Grand March Past' because the toilers march past the pay-table and receive nothing that day. The living amongst the poorest workmen will be very meagre, and a great many will not have enough to eat until the next Friday comes round bringing with it the first pay.

Decades later Jack Fleetwood who worked in the Brass Foundry also remembers this same hardship in the 1930s. Jack says:

Before 1938 the workers got no holiday pay so the first week back at work you got no wages, as when you started work you worked a week in hand. When the rent man or the Insurance man called, mother would say 'Go and tell him that I'm out.' I would go to the door and say, 'Mam said I was to tell you she's out.' He would say, 'O.K. see you next week.'

With money so tight, saving up had to be done methodically and strictly adhered to. Mrs Ivy Lawrence remembered that her family used to 'save up on the Co-op divi to pay for TRIP Week'. Many of the Shops in the factory had their own savings club. Each week the men would hand over part of their pay packet, happy in the knowledge that when the time came, they would have enough money to pay for their holiday lodgings. Mrs Jan Davis and Mr Ron Glass both have memories of their fathers doing this. Jan remembers that:

Dad would save up all year with a club at work and then on the Thursday night prior to going on Saturday he would bring his cash home. One year he fanned all the notes out in his hand and we marvelled at how much money he had as we had never seen so much! I couldn't tell you how much it was, but it was extremely hard to save like that but thanks to the 'firm' he was able to do so.

Ron talks about the sacrifice made by his dad, who was a fitter and turner in AM Shop:

My Dad used to like a smoke but from Christmas until we went away on holiday, he would pack up smoking so that he could afford to take us away, me, my Mum, and my sister. After he had finished what he was given for Christmas, that was it. There was never any Woodbines on the shopping list for the Co-Op. He would save his 1/4d a week from January til July. Working that out, those month's savings paid for the 30/- or so, and then later 35/- for rooms and attendance. That was a lot of money then, especially when you think what Dad was paid. His basic rate was about 40/- a week and then there were his extras, so he was getting about £3 2s 0d a week. That's before the war, up until about 1937 or '38. Yes, that was really a lot of money to pay out.

Another way the families saved was the 'Diddlum' Club. The first payment after Christmas was ½d. The next week 1d, and so on until it reached 6d. It would stay at that amount for the rest of the year until TRIP. To make ends meet every means of saving had to be taken. Many of the men would 'box-clever' and hang on to their bonus and overtime slips, only presenting them for payment in the week before TRIP, much to the chagrin of the company as this 'balance-week' meant even larger pay-outs than normal balance weeks. The children also did their bit, as Mrs Stella Taylor recalls of the late 1940s and '50s, 'My father paid into a TRIP fund to help finance our holiday, and I saved my pocket money in an old mustard tin with a slit in the top'.

Trevor Cockbill remembered how kindly adults would help out youngsters who were saving for TRIP:

Dressed for TRIP, 1934. Cyril Cox, aged nine, is resplendent in knickerbocker suit and cap reserved for chapel and for TRIP holidays. Cyril's Dad, Harry, was a forgeman in the Steam Hammer Shop. Cyril went late into the railways, but eventually worked as a porter on Swindon Station for twenty-five years.

how rich we were when we boarded those 'Trip' trains. Uncles, aunts and kind neighbours had called at the house, and unknown to us, dropped pennies, 'thruppenny joeys' and even 'tanners' into money boxes...

Other TRIP preparations were more fun. Clothes were a big part of TRIP – the buying of, the making of, the cleaning and the packing of clothes took a lot of attention. Even in the days of just a day trip, people still liked to treat themselves to a new outfit. Alfred Williams writes:

Whatever new clothes are bought for the summer are usually worn for the first time at 'trip.' Then the men don their new suits of shoddy, and the pinched or portly dames deck themselves out in all the glory of cheap 'fashionable' finery. The young girls are radiant with colour – white, red pink and blue and the children come dressed in brand-new garments all stiff from the warehouse.

The gentleman journalist writing about TRIP in the GWR magazine in 1903, is also very impressed with the turnout of the female travellers:

To have surveyed the attire of the fair members of the crowd would at once disabuse the mind of the idea that there is no fashion in Swindon. Despite the very early hour the fair creatures had for the most part dressed with grace and style, even to the dainty arrangement of their hair, and to survey some o' them one was tempted to wonder whether they had been to bed at all.

Mrs Mabel Harding, one of six girls, recalled the flurry of excitement around making their new clothes for TRIP in the 1890s:

After the arrival of the bale of bleached calico at home, busy fingers began on patterns and measurements for the making of our undergarments. Everyone was roped in for this business from the oldest to the youngest and all occupied in the task, from the sharpening of scissors to the turning down of hems. Many is the long seam sewn by myself, many the button holes stitched. Others would 'cut out', others would 'run and fell.' Mother meanwhile measuring and fitting and afterwards putting the finishing touches by crocheting the lace for trimming the garments. Nearer still the excitement grew, there were finishing touches to outer garments, the making of socks and stockings and last minute purchases of overalls and print dresses.

Decades later in the 1920s, '30s and '40s, Mrs Joyce Murgatroyd recalls as a small girl, her mother and her aunt making new dresses for TRIP, and then, when aged fifteen, making her own dress for TRIP. It was always important to Swindon Trippers to look smart and fashionable on TRIP, whether on a day trip, on arrival day or on the holiday Sunday, when only 'Sunday Best' would do. Mr E.R. Gill, formerly of Vilett Street, Swindon, recalls, 'Our Sunday Best clothes were always taken to wear on just that one day.'

John Edward Turner, a fourth generation railwayman who worked in the offices, remembered that the men of the 1930s liked to look smart and presentable too. John wrote:

At the time the typical railwayman's uniform would have been a navy serge suit, white plimsolls ('daps' from Woolworths costing 1s 11d and 3 farthings) an open neck shirt and a bowler hat. An occasional non-conforming wore a straw-brimmer!

In the railway factory there was a strict hierarchy for the men of which hats one could and could not wear. Bowlers were for the bosses and foremen. Flat caps were for the workers. This tradition was usually carried through into everyday life. Hats were an important item of wear, even after the Second World War. People would not leave home without one on, especially the ladies. John adds, 'The little girls wore bonnets edged with pretty pink ribbon. The women would also have been uniformly clad, wearing a best hat, possibly resembling a basket of fruit or a bird's nest!'

Later, when the holiday had grown to a week or even two, the clothes planning and preparation became even more complicated. The womenfolk would gather in and wash all the required everyday and Sunday Best clothes, days, even weeks, before the off. The consequence for the family of having to 'make do' with one set of old clothes as all others had been packed in the tin trunks or battered suit cases to be picked up by the chap on the horse and cart and sent on as 'Luggage in Advance', is one remembered by many. Mrs Margaret Suffolk recalls:

We would be so excited seeing Mum packing the large brown trunk. We had to hand over our summer clothes a couple of weeks in advanced. Mum would wash, press and pack them and send the trunk off. It was always there waiting for us to collect.

'Luggage in Advance' was a tradition that was a real godsend for the Trippers as it saved a lot of hassle on the days of departure *and* return, even if it caused a lot of hassle of 'making do' beforehand. Luggage in Advance whereby the holiday luggage was picked up and delivered to the destination addresses at the other end, was a big help for the holidaymakers but made extra work for the Parcels Department. They had to collect, label and prepare for dispatch thousands of packages going to hundreds of destinations. In the 'olden' days a horse and cart would plod around the 'Company 'ouses' to make the collection. In later years this was replaced by various vans and lorries. *The Railway Magazine* was greatly impressed by this operation. In its write-up

Above: New clothes for TRIP often meant making your own. Joyce Murgatroyd (*née* Bezer), on the right, beside her Gran Simpkins, remembers this was the first dress she made on her own for TRIP when she was aged fifteen. Her mother Agnes Bezer and sister Beryl also wear new clothes made for TRIP. Joyce remembers helping to make Beryl's hat.

Left: Ron and Dot Glass, aged twenty-eight and twenty-four, show off their new clothes in the height of fashion for 1951. Ron was very proud of this suit with its Oxford Bags. Even then, only Sunday Best would do on Sundays, even for the beach.

of TRIP in 1913, it marvels that on 8 July three van-loads, about 570 packages, were collected. The following day a similar number were loaded up. There was also a huge stack of luggage on the Milk Bank waiting to be transferred into four railway vans. In later years the luggage was despatched from Swindon Town Station in Old Town, relieving Swindon Junction of some of the workload. When talking to people about this aspect of TRIP, they would speak quite matter-of-factly about it. Never once did anyone tell me that their, or anybody else's, luggage had failed to turn up. They never doubted it would appear and it never seemed to let them down.

Luggage on the day gave an opportunity for older children, unlucky enough not to be going away on TRIP, to earn a few extra pennies. It became a tradition to hire out their 'bogies', both for the departures and the returns. Derek Benfield remembers that these handmade carts made from 'anything you could get your hands on' were particularly prized if the rear axle wheels were from a large Pedigree pram. With such a bogie you were the envy of the other children as well as a TRIP entrepreneur. This practice happened at both ends of the journey. Trippers arriving in St Ives and Tenby remember young lads there pushing their homemade bogies, hoping to make some pocket money.

As well as new clothes, a change of footwear was an essential part and long tradition of TRIP. White 'daps' for boys and men and canvas shoes for girls and ladies were an absolute must. Mr John 'Jack' Fleetwood is one of many who remembers having 'daps', 'For Trip we always had a new pair of 'daps', or 'plimsolls' as they call them now. The price for these were about 6d a pair (slightly lower if they were black).' Mrs Jean Spicer remembers:

His only pair
at
Trip

What a to do when you have to make do with just one pair of trousers until you get to your seaside destination, as all your other clothes have been packed and sent off as 'Luggage in Advance'.

Trippers waiting on the old Platform 4 of Swindon Junction Station, *c.*1912. In background can be seen the old covered footbridge traversing the mainline and linking the platforms on either side. It is sad to reflect that within a few short years some of these fine gentlemen may have departed to fight in, and not survived, the First World War.

> In those day we [ladies and girls] all wore canvas shoes for the summer. These usually had a round toe with a bar. They were either white which you blancoed or you could get some sandy coloured ones, which my mother always wore. When you blancoed, if you used milk rather than water, it stayed on a bit longer.

Swimming togs for the kids, and eventually the adults, became a vital part of TRIP packing. In early years people would sit on the beach in all their clothes — suits, dresses, jackets, shawls and hats, removing very little, if anything at all! 'Beachwear' changed dramatically over the decades and in later years, as society became more relaxed, swimsuits became more acceptable and more people 'stripped-off'.

One notable TRIP tradition, immortalised in one of a series of cartoon postcards, was the 'Annual Wash' or 'TRIP Scrub'. This was taken the night before and was an essential ritual to make sure that at least you started the holiday clean even if you did not arrive at your destination as such. In the early years it would have been a big undertaking, filling up the copper, boiling up the water and then getting all the family bathed, hair washed and dried on the same night. Some families were large, with six, seven or eight children, plus the parents, so this was no small task, but it had to be done. Mr E.R. Gill, whose family was one of these large famikies, recalls that, 'Immediately after dinner on the day before TRIP my mother started to wash and bathe all of us in turn, the youngest first and the others following in order of age. As each one was dried we were put to bed.'

One of the happy rituals loved by the children was the 'looking out of buckets and spades' and making sure they took them with them. Margaret Suffolk remembered this vividly, 'We would carry our buckets and spades while Mum and Dad carried the smaller bags down to get the train.' Mrs L.Willow also recalls these essential requirements for TRIP:

...we were all ready the night before, bathed and dressed and almost sent to bed with our shoes on. Alarms all set to wake us, bags packed, sandwiches cut and ready, bucket and spades by the front door.

For the children buckets and spades were always very much part of the excitement, as were, strangely enough, bags of paper discs and thin paper streamers. The paper game started early and was passed on down the years as remembered by a number of people interviewed. Alfred Williams remarked on this game saying that the children came equipped with 'spade and bucket and bags full of thin paper, cut the size of pennies, to throw out of the carriage windows as the train flies along.' Mr Gill and Mrs Joyce Murgatroyd remember doing this during the 1920s. Joyce and her friends spent hours cutting out circles from newspapers with the small flat discs with metal edges found in sherbert dabbers. 'We would throw the paper out of the windows creating a confetti trail for miles,' she says. 'Nobody minded then.' Decades later, other Trippers remember going on board with paper streamers which they would hang out of the windows and watch them be ripped to shreds and float away in the slipstream.

Everybody without exception remembers the nervous restlessness of the night before TRIP, followed by the exciting thrill of walking the normally empty streets in the early morning, chattering and laughing with friends and neighbours, at an hour when all good people are usually tucked up in bed. Kath Bridges remembers it very well, when she was a small girl in the 1920s.

We used to look forward to that day – only a day away. We used to be so excited about it. We used to wake up really early in the morning and look out the bedroom window even about

Platform 4, twenty years later. Trippers are waiting for the Barry Island train, one of the most consistently popular destinations. They have probably entered via the Milk Bank off Station Road, from where the early morning milk and newspaper trains departed. To the left is the Parcel Office by the gas lamp and then behind is the Telegraph Office. A siphon wagon is on the right, waiting for parcel freight.

Above and below: What a job this would have been the night before TRIP. One year the local paper told of two families travelling on TRIP, one of fifteen memebrs and one of seventeen. Imagine washing and drying that lot in one go – hair and all! (David Bedford)

Right and below: The excitement of TRIP morning is hard to imagine now. The huge numbers alone would have sparked a special kind of energy and exhilaration. Imagine walking out of Wembley after a Cup Final and your team has won. That's something like the experience of TRIP morning in its heyday. These cartoon postcards capture the experience. (David Bedford)

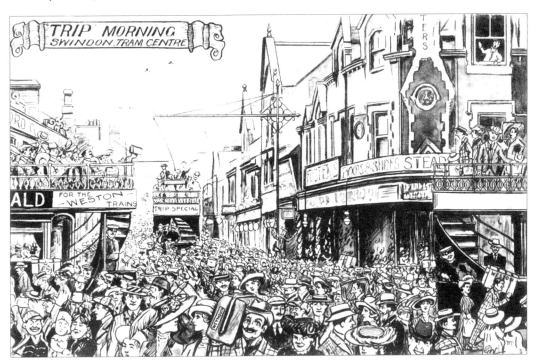

Above: Mr Sid Gibb, formerly a boilermaker in LS Shop, later promoted to foreman in L2 Tender Shop, with his wife Elsie and son Ken, paddling in the shallows at Weymouth. Elsie is very à la mode in her knitted swimsuit and hair band. Sid has daringly rolled up his trouser legs and discarded his jacket. Young Ken sports a sunhat and knitted cossie that grew down your legs when it got wet.

Left: Susan Turner, a fourth generation 'Tripper', paddles in Weymouth in the early 1950s. Susan's swimwear is more revealing and definitely less itchy than Ken Gibb's.

five o'clock in the morning. We used to say to Mum 'Oh Mum, they've started to go down to the station.' It was quite a little walk from where we lived and we would be all excited.

Mrs Elizabeth Hart's father, Thomas Hanks, worked as a boilermaker in the Boiler Shop. Elizabeth remembers making that walk as a small child in the 1930s:

We lived in Montagu Street so walked to the station. It was difficult for us to try to be quiet. I remember walking up Jenning Street and hearing someone snoring very loudly.

Jack Fleetwood, too, has vivid memories of this early morning walk. He says:

I can remember walking down Regent Street with crowds of other people… All the neighbours would walk down together. There would be a lot of chattering and laughing from the children even though we set off from home at about 5.30 a.m. to get a good place on the train. When you got to the gates Tommy King would be there selling his home-made boiled sweets.

Perhaps the most eloquent description of this walk is given by Trevor Cockbill. Trevor wrote:

… early in the morning, we were roused, dressed in our 'Sunday Best' and marshalled ready for the tramp through dark streets to the point of embarkation. Many of us proceeded past the 'Company's 'ouses' and The Park to the end of Dean Street, then up the sloping ramp at the side of Rodbourne Road bridges, where special 'Trip Trains' for West of England resorts had been marshalled and were waiting. By the time we reached Park Lane the families which had been walking in the darkness on the other side of the road, or just ahead of us, or just behind us, merged with others at each street corner so the road and the pavements were full of shuffling people. Parents strove to keep their children quiet, but the noise was then considerable. People who had walked some distance paused to plonk down heavy cases, seaside spades were trailed and made a scraping noise along the pavements, seaside buckets chinked and clinked, rubber balls were 'dapped' and caught, or in the darkness missed and lost… and every now and then an exasperated parent hissed 'Johnnie pick that spade up!' 'Peggie, another squeak from you my girl and home you go at once!'

One of the greatest excitements of all, especially for the children, was getting onto the train, with its big smoking, steaming engine, not from the platform in the train station as one would normally do, but somewhere much more exciting, down in the sidings, usually Rodborne sidings. Trevor Cockbill again captures that feeling:

at last the excitement, the feeling of a very special privilege as we were allowed to climb the steps, into a railway carriage, *not from the platform* but from the cinder-strewn Trackside… *because we were real railway people.*

Many others remember this special privilege, too. They talk of the sense of pride and belonging they felt as they stood amongst the sounds of hissing engines, the smells of coal and steam, and the dirt and grit of the sidings. Sylvia Houghton recalls that feeling:

It was a wonderful feeling going up ..and seeing all the trains lined up with their destination printed across them… to a child they looked so big with all the steam coming out. We were told to stand well back and hold hands. Then we'd go onto this wonderful thing that our father had helped to make.

Mary Starley (*née* Rudduck) is proud of her TRIP photos. This is one with her grandparents in 1919, on Tenby beach. From left to right, back row: Mrs Reid, -?-, Mrs Sarah Rudduck, Doris, Sarah's daughter aged sixteen years. On the left is Mr Ralph, a great friend of the family. On the right is Mr George Rudduck. This carefully arranged group trying to look casually posed are obviously dressed in their Sunday Best. The two older boys wear smart sailor suits, the little lads elaborate, embroidered collars. The women have decorated hats. The men look debonair with straw boaters and Mr Ralph even sports flowers in his lapel. It is difficult to picture this stylish group as hard labouring, working-class railwaymen. Mary Starley's Grandpa Rudduck was troubled with a stiff leg from an accident in the Works, yet manages to look 'a gay spark' here, as Mary says.

Climbing up the wooden steps into the carriage was a daunting prospect for little children. For Mrs Mollie Saunders, those wooden steps and the ride on the train are her strongest memories of TRIP. She says, 'Perhaps the memory that stands out most is the long ladder which we had to climb to get into the trains. Although there were many railway helpers, I was always a little afraid of falling'. This was not an unreasonable worry as the steps had no handrails and were rather steep. For children struggling up with buckets and spades, or mothers with picnic bags, or small children, it was quite a challenge. Mollie goes on to say, 'I remember that sometimes we would have a comfortable seat in the train and some years we had to sit on the floor or sit in the toilet and it was rather cramped and uncomfortable. We didn't care. We were carrying buckets and spades and ready to go'.

Hundreds of coaches went into making up TRIP Trains. These needed to be gathered from all over the region. Older, less used stock would be set aside, standing, waiting patiently, gathering dust for weeks or even months in the sidings. Jack Fleetwood remembers the dreadful state of the seats in the coaches and how the children were given express instructions of what *not* to do!

We were forbidden to bang the seats on the train as clouds of dust would come out, as these coaches had been parked in sidings for months. When we got in the coach we were nice and clean, but when we got to Weston we would be mucky, so Mather carried soap and flannel for a clean-up.

In the days of non-corridor coaches there would be the obvious problems regarding calls of nature. For some young lads this presented an opportunity that perhaps would not have been allowed at other times, i.e. peeing out of the window. Some even remember it turning into a bit of a competition, a highlight of the journey, year on year! For girls and lads of more modest dispositions, the sandcastle buckets came in handy as Jack Fleetwood vividly recalls, 'On one occasion we went to Weston in a non-corridor coach with gas lamps and wooden slatted seats. With five of us children, the buckets came in handy!' Comfort stops, or what were then called LPs, 'Lavatory Purposes', were built into the itinerary and the Trippers would form orderly long queues for the toilets at the stations. Station toilet facilities were not built with such numbers in mind and so it was a long wait and an ultra quick pee before hopping back onboard again. Later, even when in corridor coaches, it was not easy, as Mr John Mudge, who started as an office boy in the Works in AM Shop in 1956, recalls of his trips down to St Ives. Although technically there was supposed to be a seat per person, John remembers, 'Many people spent the night on suitcases in the corridors. Great fun when you needed the loo in the night!'.

Waiting early in the morning in the railway sidings without any means of shelter could indeed be great fun, or pure misery, depending on the weather conditions – sunshine,

Compare this 1950s family group of Mary and friends to that of her grandparents in 1919. How times have changed. How much more relaxed they all look and what a lot of flesh they are showing – one even wearing a daring two-piece swimsuit! From left to right: Mrs Richardson, Mary Starley, her friend Joan, Dot Glass and Mr and Mrs Glass Senior, who always went on TRIP together.

Foreman and clerks and managers were lucky enough to have compartments reserved for everybody else it was first come, first served, so everyone tried to get there first.

Every Tripper was, in theory, allocated a seat on a train. In reality, many families and friends squeezed in all together as can be seen in this humorous depiction of a full-up TRIP compartment. The notice says, 'To Seat Five' so there should be only ten. How many can you count?

drenching rain and even fog on one occasion. Writing of the 1900 Record TRIP in *The Railway Magazine* in 1901, the writer remarks that, 'fog came on during the period of embarking' and was 'very dense for some little time and many of trains had to be slowed up on account of it'. Some canny workers found a way around this hanging about. Mrs Clarice Baddeley remembers how, back in the early 1900s:

> Dad was a coach maker and he always managed to have the key to one of the train coaches, which meant that when we arrived at the siding of the station at about 5 a.m. we didn't have to wait to be let on the train. Dad would simply unlock one of the carriages and up we would all go!²

No seats were allocated and it was important to make your claim to a carriage early, in order for the family to be all together. Frank Saunders remembers the fun of being stuffed in:

> We used to cram into the carriage. My Dad use to say to us little 'uns 'stick your noses up against the window and nobody will want to come in with us'... mind you it was nearly full with just us lot... seven of us there were and our Mam and Dad like.

Sylvia Houghton remembers her family's strange sleeping practice back in the 1920s and how surprisingly soothing it was:

> My two youngest sisters were put up on the luggage rack and tied with a belt to sleep. The seats went right across the carriage and with the blinds pulled down we could all lie down and sleep to the motion that only comes from a steam train.

Ivy Lawrence recalled the same experience a decade later:

> We used to climb up where the luggage went and go to sleep. It wasn't comfortable, but it was always packed in our carriage, so Dad would say 'up you go and sleep' and we would sleep till we got there.

Mrs Mary Starley remembers TRIP Trains for a completely different reason. Her grandfather, George Rudduck, had a disability. This made it very difficult for him to travel anywhere, especially on public transport. Mary remembers how important TRIP was to him and the family:

> He had an accident when he was working in the factory and his leg was left stiff. He couldn't get about much 'cos his leg wouldn't bend. Imagine what it was like having a stiff leg stuck out like that all the time. You would be in people's way. He couldn't go in a bus or any thing like that. Well.you know what trains were like in those days with corridors in the coaches -so in the railway carriage he could sit this side and put his leg up on the other seat and not bother anyone. It was great for him. It meant he could go away.

Once in the train and going, John Turner remembered the thrill of the journey spent counting off the stations all the way down to Weymouth – Swindon, Wootton Bassett, Chippenham, Thingley Junction, Trowbridge, Westbury, Clink Road Junction, Blatchbridge Junction, Castle Cary, Yeovil (PenMill), Yetminster, Maiden Newton, Dorchester West, and finally Weymouth. The Specials were heavy trains and did not go that fast. 'Dad, how fast are we going', was a question often asked by Derek Benfield of his father and his dad would know, because he was that wonderful thing, an engine driver. Most of the GWR locos had no speedometers in

the cab at that time (c.1930s) so the driver would take out his watch and count the number of telegraph poles passed within a certain time. It was a good method and became standard practice for drivers. They needed to be good at it as being on time was, to quote Derek, 'an essential requisite for GWR'.

Whilst some vividly remember the time the TRIP journey took or the speed that the trains travelled down the track, Mr Ronald Clack recalls an event in 1928 when the train was stopped on the line. It has to be remembered, and this is one of the amazing parts of TRIP, that TRIP Specials were always run in such a way as to not interfere with normal traffic working; therefore, TRIP Trains would be halted to allow normal traffic flow. Ronald and his family were on a Special bound for Weymouth but it had halted, waiting for a regular train to pass through. Ronald, aged eight years, and his young friend Vic Baker, were restless as this was not the first time the train had stopped. They were playing with the door handle when Vic managed to unlatch it and it suddenly swung wide open, with Ronald hanging on. He hung on for dear life, dangling over the adjacent track, but he could not hang on long enough for the adults to close the door and eventually he dropped down onto the dirt below. Luckily, his dad, Hubert, a wagon builder, was a nimble man. Knowing what dangerous places railway lines are and that an express would soon be passing, he speedily leapt down, swooped young Ron up and literally threw him up back into the carriage, clambering up after him as quickly as he could. Leaning out and pulling in the carriage door was a bit tricky, but they just managed it when the express came thundering by, right on the spot where young Ron had fallen. Ron and Vic learnt a valuable lesson about door handles that day and lived to follow their grandfathers and fathers into the Works. Ron became a coach painter and Vic ended up as an Instructor in the Training School. Another line-side incident is recalled by Mrs Pam Collier whilst on a TRIP Special to Margate in the 1950s: 'I remember the train breaking down and all the men got off the train to try to help mend it. The wives were not too happy with their husbands then getting back into the train with their white shirts now covered in grease, soot and dirt.' Happily, these events ended safely and did not blot the copybook for TRIP's safety record.

Food provision and food treats were another of the customs of TRIP that have passed into its folklore. Arriving at Swindon Station and queuing to buy 1d or 2d worth of boiled homemade sweets from Tommy King was the first of these tasty pleasures. Cutting chunky bread slices to make doorstop sandwiches to see you through the day, or maybe the journey, well, at least to Wootton Bassett, was another one. Faggots and peas on a freezing cold day at Weston, enormous

Opposite above: Trippers make their way to the trains in the sidings. It would appear that these Trippers had already had their breakfast and, maybe, lunchtime sandwiches, from the amount of litter around the place, or it may be that the children had already started scattering their paper discs and streamers prepared for TRIP.

Opposite below: A host of early risers make their way alongside the Carriage Works in the vicinity of the sawmills to their waiting train. Interestingly, almost everyone without exception is hatted. Bowler hats, flat caps and trilbys for the men, caps for the boys, cloche type hats for the women and bonnets for the girls. The longcoated, capped railway official gentleman is deep into lighting his pipe. Does he know he has wandered into the railway tracks? Dave Ellis, who was involved in the working of TRIP between 1947 and 1952, remembers that, on TRIP morning, a special entrance was opened by the Timber Stores, opposite the present Pattern Stores public house, which was manned by Head Office or Divisional Ticket Inspectors.

Above: TRIP 1934. Passengers boarding their train alongside No.6 Carriage Shop on what looks to have been a rather 'cool' morning judging by the number of people wearing overcoats. These coaches would have had toilet facilities but they are showing their age being of a type known as 'Toplights' (after the top lights or little glasses positioned above the main windows). They were some of Churchward's earlier designs being built in quantity from 1904. These coaching stock have no lower footboards so ladders have been procured from No.11 Shop nearby. Many Trippers have special memories of climbing up these little wooden steps, which seemed so big to little people. Note the young man with his hand in his pockets in holiday mode wearing his TRIP daps. (Brian Arman)

Left: Francis John Bastin, pattern maker and design draftsman, remembers the fun and games of trying to get up into the trains with or without the little wooden steps. He says: 'only a limited number of steps were available for boarding the train from the permanent way. Impatient to get a good seat and not in possession of steps resulted in ladies of all shapes and sizes being unceremoniously hauled aboard. The indignant shrieks from some and the good-natured giggles from others as their men pulled or pushed any part of the anantomy available was something (even at five years old) I shall always treasure.'

Cornish pasties and apple pie and cream made by the landladies, a first taste of cornflakes, a sand-flecked ice cream from the ice-cream man, a tea tray on the beach, so many different memories. Having a fish-and-chip supper all to yourself was an expensive treat, beyond normal, everyday living, and to be remembered with lip-licking appreciation. Mr Frank Saunders recalls that his family's day trip to Weston always ended with this fabulous treat.

> It were smashing on the way back. We'd all have fish and chips. Yeah, they would save up so that we could all have one. That was no mean thing with us being so many. [seven children] Ooh that were a real treat. I can remember them now. Tasted ever so good they did.

The overriding food tradition of TRIP was in association with the accommodation. Swindon trippers could not afford to stay in hotels. They stayed in 'ordinary houses'. However, the arrangement they had with the landladies was not bed and breakfast as we know it today, but 'Rooms and Attendance'. Mrs Kath Bridges explains:

> Then it was rooms and attendance. You used to pay for a room and buy your own food and the landlady would cook it for you. I remember we would book a room or two, and go out and buy what we wanted, fish or Cornish pasties - or she would make them for you. They would cook what you bought, what you wanted. If you didn't have much money, you didn't buy much.

Other means of making the money stretch and still provide a good meal were also employed. Many railwaymen grew their own vegetables; come TRIP they would dig them up, take them with them and give them over to the landlady to cook during their holiday week. Mrs Mabel Harding remembers preparations to ensure the family had enough food for the holiday very clearly:

> The baking of a huge dough cake, the boiling of a large ham and later the shelling of peas and picking over of fruit. Butter was wrapped in cabbage leaves, soft fruit likewise and all placed carefully in the food box in order to supplement the week's supply.

Rooms and Attendance also meant that the landlady would clean and tidy up your rooms for you as remembered by Ivy Lawrence; 'We use to have what they called "rooms and attendance" where the landlady would do all the work and the cooking and cleaning for us... we didn't have to do any work at all. Lovely!'

TRIP holidays had all the usual seaside ingredients of sand, sea and, hopefully, sun, but for John Turner's family, as well as for others, it also meant:

> Merry-go-rounds, ice creams, donkey rides, sailing ships and steamers, red-coated bandsmen with great silver blowing trumpets, the Salvation Army holding meetings on the sands, Mr Punch and a vaudeville, lobster teas at Osmington Mills and mechanical toast racks that plied their way from the King's Statue to Bowleaze Cove.

For Swindon Trippers it also entailed specially organised sports days, sandcastle competitions, cricket matches against the local team, singing contests, shows and carnivals, sometimes organised by the locals, sometimes by the Trippers themselves. Ivy Lawrence remembered how her uncle would set to in St Ives and get the children organised.

> My uncle, Mr. Dunsford, he would organise races and things on the beach for the Swindon children. He made it good fun. He'd buy little things for prizes like to give us, you know sweets and things.

Susan Turner rides the merry-go-round at Weymouth. Merry-go-rounds are one of the traditional features of a seaside resort and memories of TRIP. You can see one behind the Dickson family in their photo taken at Exmouth.

Not surprisingly, the beach was *the* essential ingredient in the holiday. It was where they spent the greatest part of every day. Talk to any Tripper and they will tell you that one of the 'highly desirables' of TRIP holiday was their own little beach hut, or, before huts, a beach tent. No matter which seaside resort they went to – Paignton, St Ives, Exmouth, Weymouth or Margate – a beach tent or hut was a must. Families and friends who worked together in the factory or office, or lived next door to each other, would go off together and have beach huts nextdoor to each other, year after year. The extended Bezer family and friends booked a run of beach tents for many years for their week in Weymouth during the 1920s and '30s. Mrs Joyce Murgatroyd recalls that her mother remembered that one year they arrived at their tent to find it full of Swindon day trippers sheltering from the heavy rain. They kindly let them stay, but on their return the next day were dismayed to find the sand inside the tent covered in shrimp shells. The beach huts were practical and a blessing in many ways, as Ron Glass remembers:

My workmates were going down to Margate. So that was it. That's where we were going too. He was a Coppersmith and his wife and two children, my wife and I, a boilermaker, his wife and daughter and my pal's sister, her husband and three children. We all went on the holiday train to Margate. It was like having an extended family really. You were with your workmates

Above: An older, grey-whiskered Grandpa George Rudduck in Penzance around the 1930s, enjoying an ice-cream treat with his young neighbours from Hunters Grove, Renee and Sonny Hatt. The ice-cream seller was known to Trippers as 'Okey-Poky' the ice-cream man.

Right: Donkey and horse rides were a feature of TRIP popular with the youngsters. Susan Murgatroyd takes a ride in St Ives.

Above: The Bezer family always booked a run of beach tents on Weymouth beach. Joyce and little Beryl Bezer sit in front of their family. From left to right, back row: Uncle Ernest Simpkins, Dad, Ewart Bezer, Uncle Ernie Greenwood. Front row: Aunt Cath Simpkins, Mum, Agnes Bezer, Aunt Lou Greenwood.

Left: It is 1951 and Mrs Hilda Glass celebrates her birthday which always fell in the first few days of TRIP holiday. It became a tradition for family and friends to decorate her hut, Beach Hut No.1, on Preston Sands, Paington. One of the messages reads, 'Mine's a Pint'.

Here, Mary Starley's father, George Rudduck, a fitter in A Shop, celebrates his forty-eighth birthday, also in 1951. His birthday was just a couple of days after Hilda Glass's. The message says 'Many Happy Returns to George.' George's family always had Beach Hut No.2 next door to Hilda Glass.

all the week and then you went on holiday with them, but it was that sort of community. We all had beach huts along the front. We had 3 beach huts. If it happened to be raining the men would get in one beach hut playing cards, the ladies used to get in another one sewing and nattering and all the children in the last beach hut.

One romantic tradition that developed over the years was the practice of using TRIP for that extra-special holiday. Many young railway couples planned their weddings for just before TRIP holiday. TRIP made a grand honeymoon. In later years the local paper would be full of wedding announcements and pictures. Mrs Jan Ward's uncle, Harry Bruton, a coachmaker, and his bride Rene, who had worked at Will's factory, travelled out of the GWR system to Scarborough for their honeymoon in 1924. Their families thought that was very daring!

That TRIP held a special magic for those who went on it is obvious from the warm and affectionate way they talk of it, from the fond memories they still have of it, and the fact that those memories still burn so brightly for them.

1. Mrs Enid Saunders in interview
2. *The Evening Advertiser*, 22 March 1986

CHAPTER THREE

DESTINATIONS

The first TRIP destination was Oxford, but the second TRIP was to Torquay and so began the Trippers' love affair with the seaside. In early times the choice of places to go to was restricted to anywhere along the Great Western Railway routes. Over the decades as the GWR spread all over the western region and Wales, new destinations were added. Later, through special arrangements with other railway companies' Trippers could travel all over the country. Eventually, Trippers even travelled abroad to Ireland and the Continent. The list of TRIP destinations grew to be an incredibly long one. At its height it could run to 350 different places. Most favoured were the seaside resorts. This is not at all surprising when one considers the contrasting environments. Swindon was dirty, gritty, noisy and industrial, while the seaside was clean, fresh, invigorating and picturesque. On TRIP there was time to just sit and look out to the horizon at the blue of the waves, the yellow of the sand or the green of the surrounding countryside. No wonder the Swindonians fell in love with these wonderful places.

All of those who went on TRIP recall wonderful times. Only after they have been talking for some time, and then only after gently prodding, do they own up to the possibility that TRIP wasn't always sunshine and laughter, and that temperamental thing, the English weather, could make for a less than happy time. In both Weymouth and St Ives locals recall that Swindon folk had a tradition of bringing the rain with them. In 1908 the *Southern Times* reported that the organisers of TRIP could not have chosen a 'more unfortunate day' as it rained practically the whole of the day. It describes how the Trippers utilised 'every conceivable form of shelter to its fullest capacity', and many hundreds of them spent most of the morning hanging around the station. What a disappointment for Trippers and traders alike as a record number went to Weymouth that year, 3,121 adults and 3,050 children, making a grand total of 6,171. Ken Gibbs, a fourth generation railwayman and author of *Swindon Works – Apprentice in Steam*, remembers that holidays decades later in the 1930s could sometimes be just like that:

One TRIP we seemed to spend sheltering from the rain on the beach under the pier or wandering around sheltering in shop doorways or under shop awnings. Sometimes, knowing the landlady so well, we were allowed to stay in doors, but it was often, with some landladies, that the visitors were expected to be out of the house after breakfast only returning during the day for the midday meal and for tea.

Jack Fleetwood also remembers a day of rain on their precious day trip:

One year when we got to Weston it was pouring with rain. The womenfolk saw the stationmaster and asked if they could stay on the train with the children. He agreed to have the

Clean, fresh air was not something Swindon was noted for in its early industrial beginnings. The seaside air would clear the head and make one feel much better.

Fresh air and wonderful scenery captivated the Trippers. Little Jan Ward (*née* Cox) sits on Grandma Marion Bruton's lap. Standing is her mother, Marion Cox, who worked in the Wages Office. Uncle Seth Bruton, a tool maker, stares back at his father, Harry Bruton, coachmaker, who is taking the photograph on TRIP 1937.

No matter what the weather, Swindon Trippers were determined to get on the beach. Mother Fleetwood, daughter Irene, Irene's husband David and little Pat, button up and brave it out on the sands at Weymouth during the 1950s.

train shunted into a bay which had a platform and we sat there all day. The train toilets were locked, so we had to get out and use those on the station.

Mather went and got some chips to go with our sandwiches. We started for home about 6 p.m. and never even saw the sea.

Whatever the weather, the Trippers were determined to enjoy themselves and make the most of their break.

That other temperamental character of an English seaside holiday could also make or break their stay: the Bed & Breakfast landlady. It was a TRIP tradition for families to return year after year not only to the same resort but also to the same lodgings. Mr E.R. Gill, whose father was a mechanic, remembers staying seventeen times in the same lodgings in Wesley Street, Weymouth. Happily, most families, like Mr Gill's and Lorna Dawes' family, were fortunate to have good relationships with their landladies, but some were not so lucky. The caricature of the bad-tempered harridan could be found in many of the lodgings taken over by the Trippers. Mrs Stella Taylor has strong memories of her lodgings in Weymouth in the late 1940s and early 1950s:

We used to stay at a boarding house in Brownlow Street, run by a Mrs C. whose daughter was a teacher at Weymouth Grammar School. We would supply groceries from our rations. Mrs C. prepared the meals. She spent her afternoons in her beach hut by the sea front. On rainy days she would glower around the front room where guests were making the best of it and say 'I don't know why you people don't go and enjoy some sea air!' She also complained if we children went upstairs during the day, as we would wear out her stair carpet − an illogical claim as it was covered with tough whitish fabric to prevent any soiling or wear. My parents swapped sides in their bed each night as the uncomfortable mattress rendered sleep on one side very difficult. However, a change of lodgings did not occur to them as Mrs C. had 'been recommended' by someone at Swindon Works!

YEAR	TO WEYMOUTH	TO WESTON	% POPULARITY OF RESORTS
1892	4524	1972	35.6%
1903	5302	3160	37.5%
1904	5698	3752	32.8%
1905	5420	3807	37.8%
1925	6000	4000	54.5%
1932	5050	4320	36.0%
1933	4559	3606	31.4%
1936	5400	3200	31.9%

The list shows that over the period of eight years, Weston and Weymouth grabbed a high percentage of Trippers.

Of all the TRIP destinations, undoubtedly Weymouth was the favourite, closely followed by Weston-super-Mare. Year upon year they were the most popular choices. Even in the 1960s they were the two most favoured destinations. Many families would start with a day out at Weston or Weymouth and then, when they could afford longer stays, would extend their holiday in these resorts, or, having grown tired of the place, move onto somewhere else. Mrs Kath Bridges had such an experience.

Weston and Weymouth, that was the two places that Swindon people went to. There were crowds on the station. I've never liked Weston much when I was older, but we did then. I think that it was going to Weston so much when we were younger, I think that we got a bit fed-up with it. Later Jim would say to me 'Have a day away', I'd say 'Oh not Weston'. You got so fed-up with it – Weston and Weymouth.

Weymouth

Weymouth, which had been popular with King George III, was also popular with Swindonians, so much so that it became known in Swindon and in Weymouth as 'Swindon-by-the-Sea'. In Weymouth the arrival day was known as 'Swindon Day', followed by 'Swindon Week'. The first TRIP Special came to Weymouth in 1870 carrying 1,000 Trippers. In 1892, 4,524 went there. It hit an all-time high of 6,171 in 1908 and a good 6,000 in 1925. In 1931 4,575 Trippers made up of 2,244 adults and 2,331 children travelled in four Special Trains. Each train was made up of fifteen coaches – thirteen Thirds and two Brake Thirds. Thirds were third-class corridor stock. They had eight compartments, each able to carry eight passengers. Brake Thirds had less compartments but had a Guard and Luggage facility. In 1936 the numbers rose to 5,400 but by 1953 they had dropped to 1,127. In 1898 the *Southern Times* had written, 'Weymouth has always been a favourite resort to the great industrial army who serve the Great Western Railway'. In 1932, under the heading 'Swindon invades Weymouth', it reported that 26,000 Swindon Trippers were holidaying in 325 places around the coast, and 'over a quarter of them have come to Weymouth'.

A happy family group in front of the beach tents they used to hire on Weymouth beach for TRIP. From left to right, back row: Ewie Bezer, Lesley Plimley, Charlie Richards, Ernie Greenwood, Grandpa Albert Simpkins. Middle row: Agnes Bezer, Edie Plimley, Annie Simpkins, Mrs Maidment, Mr. Maidment. Front row: Maidie ?, Joyce Bezer, Jean Plimley, Beryle Bezer, Roy Maidment.

There are many Swindonians with fond memories of TRIP holidays in Weymouth. It was popular with Mrs Stella Taylor's family. She says, 'It was a great favourite. On Weymouth sea front we would often meet people we knew – half Swindon was there for the week.'

Ken Gibbs also has very clear memories of times there as a young lad with his mother and father, Sid, who worked in L2 and B.B. Shop, and with their next door neighbours, who were more like an uncle and aunt to him. Ken writes:

My first experience of TRIP was at the age of about one year. For the next seven years we went to Weymouth, always to the same address. We stayed with Mrs Gage, at 81 Walpole Street. Out of the station, turn left, along the road, turn right. From the later years I can still see my father carrying two large suitcases, resting and changing hands now and again. Our larger cases had been sent ahead, 'luggage in advance'.

Mrs Gage, the landlady, was a widow. I have no idea how old she was but she reminded me of my grandmother. We had the front room of the house. In the sitting room, on the wall behind the door, was a huge framed picture of the Royal Naval Fleet Review, lines and lines of warships all named underneath. At the end of the entrance hall was the sitting room used by Mrs Gage. Over the years we got to know her well and I used to go through and talk to her. I always tried to make her laugh. She had false teeth which were loose and when she laughed her top set dropped down with a 'click' onto the bottom set. Fascinating for a small boy!

Every morning we went to the beach, back for a cooked mid-day meal, then beach again in the afternoon. We never went to the beach after tea. We would have a walk in the evening. In my early years the walk was to feed the swans and then as I got older a walk along the harbour to look at the Nothe Fort. Walking along the front was like walking in Swindon shopping centre, as everyone seemed to know everyone.

William, 'Bill' Durbidge's maternal grandfather, Fred Selwood, was a wheelwright in the Works, so Bill and his mother got to go on TRIP. Bill remembers that at Weymouth Station, 'we had to cross the lines by way of an iron girder bridge'. Here they are paddling at Weymouth in the late 1920s.

Ken Gibb, aged about three in the early 1930s, strolls confidently across the sands with neighbour 'Uncle' Frank Cottrell who worked 'Inside' as a labourer in A Erecting Shop. Frank has made some concession to the hot weather and the beach – he has rolled up his shirt sleeves and trouser legs!

Above: Walking was a great TRIP pasttime. These people are out for a stroll along Weymouth front where in 1958, you could 'meet half of Swindon.' Mr Jack Fleetwood Senior, a tractor driver in the Works, never normally wore a tie, but liked to don his best suit, best cap and his only tie on TRIP holiday. Here we see him carrying the picnic bag alongside Mrs Fleetwood who pushes her granddaughter. Next is daughter Dorothy, then John Fleetwood, and in front John's niece Pat and his sister Irene. Behind the group are the two sons-in-law, David on the left and Bill who also worked 'Inside', with Ali, John's wife tucked alongside.

Left: Diane Turner's granddad, Mr Sam Smith, wife Ada and their daughter Iris, aged about eighteen, and the dog. Any dog going on TRIP had to have its own ticket which had to be applied for along with those for bicycles and perambulators. Details available for 1954 show that G. White paid 6s 8d for his dog's ticket whilst A.J.T. Everett paid 13s 4d for his four-legged friend.

Trippers strolling in Weymouth whilst the locals go about their usual business. Note the mother with the school-boy on the left. Swindon schools would break-up early for TRIP. From left to right: Ernie Greenwood, in daps, wife Louie, Kath Simpkins, Agnes Bezer and husband Ewart.

Mrs Diane Shaw's family have a long GWR heritage and a long love affair with Weymouth that passed down through the generations until, eventually, her father moved his young family to live there. Great-grandfather John Spackman lived in Reading Street in the railway village in 1865. Her paternal grandfather, Charles Andrew Turner (born 1882) was a foreman in the Works and her maternal grandfather, Samuel Henry Smith (born 1891) was a boilermaker. Her father, John Edward Turner (born 1919), went into the Drawing Office. The family's photograph album shows their long association with TRIP holidays taken in Weymouth. Even after her father had left the Works and they had moved to Weymouth, Diane's family would always go to the station to meet TRIP Trains and greet her Uncle Nobby Morse and Aunt Minnie who also always took their holiday in Weymouth.

WESTON-SUPER-MARE

Since 1868 Weston, as it is commonly known, was a much chosen day-trip destination for Swindon Trippers. The second largest number of Trippers would choose Weston-super-Mare as their destination. Its popularity was mainly because Trippers could get quickly to the seaside, have a good long day there, and then return home feeling as if they had been on a proper holiday. The Weston trains would depart early in the morning as Mrs Millicent Cox remembers of the early 1900s, 'We had to get up very early in the morning. We left at 5.30 and got there at 7 in the morning and we left at about 8 at night'. In 1931 the Weston trains were still leaving early in the morning. The first train, No.25, left at 6.15 a.m. and arrived at 7.55 a.m. No.27 left at 6.35 a.m. followed by No.29 at 6.50 a.m. The last train, No.31, left at 7.05 a.m. and arrived at 8.55 a.m. The four trains conveyed between them 2,228 adults and 1,197 excited children.

The Trippers would depart in high spirits and with high hopes of seeing the sea, hopes which were often not fulfilled. Sadly, despite all the attractions to be found at Weston, such as the Grand

Above: Diane Shaw's TRIP family album covers five decades and four generations from 1914 up to the 1960s. This card was sent to Mr Samuel Smith, Diana Shaw's grandfather who worked as a boilermaker and lived at 70 Montague Street. The message on the back says, *We are having a grand time here, today has been cold. What do you think of our James at back. We are being photographed all day long. Alec thinks it is fine and is out often every meal.* Alec was the son of granny Ada's (Diane's grandmother) sister, Daisy.

Left: Decades later in 1958, fourth generation Trippers Diane, on the right, and her sister Susan, lean on the deckchair in which their mother sits, on Weymouth beach. From the jackets and cardigans they are wearing, it looks as if the Swindonians have brought the cool weather with them once again.

A group of Trippers exiting Weston-super-Mare Station, c.1960s. They have obviously just arrived, possibly on TRIP Wednesday, and are setting off to the beach with their picnic bags and beach ball. Note the smoke box and the chimney of the steam loco standing in the station.

Pier, the Winter and Italian Gardens, the fantastic swimming pool and the donkey rides, what Weston is most commonly known and remembered for is that it is often 'all mud and no water'. Indeed, it is the muddy sand, and getting filthy on it, that most Trippers talk about, albeit with fond amusement, as Mrs Kath Bridges evocatively recalls:

> At Weston we used to play in the mud, you couldn't call it sand could you? I can remember getting filthy. It was so muddy there. We used to come back filthy. You hardly ever saw the sea.

This is also a memory of Councillor Derek Benfield:

> … being Weston the sea was invariably out, so we would find pools of water to play in. The mud was everywhere and we always managed to bring plenty home with us!

Despite this, Derek always remembers it as, 'the magical Day Trip to Weston'. A day away was all his family, and many others, could afford. This made Weston especially attractive for the financially hard-pressed Trippers as a trip to Weston would only cost a very little, or even nothing at all, as the Swindon families would make sure to take their own drinks and picnics. Mrs Cox recalls:

> We took our own food, bread and margarine. You had to be very well off to go into the shops. Fish and chips or faggots and peas were about 4d. One year we were so desperate, it was so cold, we went into one of these shops and had faggots and peas.

1932. Ten-year-old John 'Jack' Fleetwood takes on the world, or at least the muddy sand at Weston-super-Mare. Little did he know he would grow up and become an expert on sand.

By the 1930s the bread and margarine had given way to marmite and tomato for Derek Benfield's family. He remembers that any of the sandwiches that had managed not to be eaten by lunchtime had by then turned into 'a soggy mess'.

The practice of take-your-own would not have endeared them to the shopkeepers and café owners of Weston at all. However, the pubs still did a good trade as Swindon railwaymen were always fond of a pint, especially when on their holiday, as Jack Fleetwood recalls:

The shop keepers were not very keen on Swindon people as we would take our own food and drink. The only ones to gain were the pubs, as the menfolk would see the family settled on the beach and then head off for a drink.

Mr Frank Saunders' family was another that always went to Weston for the day when he was young. Like Derek's, it was all they could afford. Frank also remembers this strange ritual of heading off for a drink:

Mind you its funny, no matter where they go these railwaymen they always have to 'see someone'. About 11 o'clock they'd all be saying to the wives... 'I've got to see someone' and off they'd head to the pub. Always the same one each year mind you. They'd be in there for a couple or three hours and then they'd come back all merry like. That was the signal for the women... they'd leave the men in charge and go up town for a bit of shopping and a look around. My Dad would sit us all down on the beach and sing us a song or two. We'd have a play for a bit and then he'd have a kip.

Weston, despite being often without its sea, won hands down for building sandcastles. Jack Fleetwood says, 'when we got to the seaside it was a mad dash for the beach, as if you went to Weston you could make very good sandcastles' and Jack should know – he spent forty-seven years of his working life working with sand in the Brass Foundry!

PAIGNTON

Paignton, Teignmouth and Torquay, called 'the English Riviera' by the GWR, all became favourite destinations for many TRIP families. Paignton, a traditional family resort, was a special favourite with many Swindonians. There is a traditional pier with amusements arcade, Paignton Green, ideal for picnics, games, and donkey rides and there are the ever-popular beach huts. Trippers were spoilt for choice between Paignton or Preston's long sandy beaches. The Murgatroyd family returned to Paignton beaches over many years and enjoyed times there with local friends, the Doran family.

The families of Mr Ron Glass and Mrs Mary Starley, *née* Rudduck, and their friends, the Goldsmiths and the Richardsons, all went to Paignton for many years. Each year they would hire a run of beach huts on Preston beach and set up a home-from-home next door to each other. Ron says:

> In 1947 my mother and father decided to go to Paignton. It was just a ordinary house we stayed in. We couldn't afford a hotel. We had a recommendation from a lady in Willis Avenue. We stayed at Preston beach.
>
> My parents had a beach hut. Beach Hut No.1. My Dad always used to book up for the following year the last day we were on holiday. We used to pay somewhere about 10/- a week. Its gone up a lot, now its about £30 a week. They were just a basic hut with a bench seat at the back. You could keep your bits in there. They were a very useful thing because if it happened to rain you could sit in there by the sea and still get the fresh air and if it happened to be sunny and you wanted to swim, you had your own changing accommodation without struggling under the towel on the beach.

TRIP was always a special holiday for the Rudduck and Glass families as both Ron's mum, Hilda, and Mary's dad, George, celebrated their birthdays soon after arrival. It became a tradition to decorate their respective beach huts with balloons, crêpe paper and little birthday messages and to celebrate with a tray of tea and buttered rolls.

ST IVES

Weymouth was not the only place that had its 'Swindon Week' – St Ives did, too. St Ives' people called the Trippers 'Swindoners', although they called themselves Swindonians, but between fishermen and railwaymen there grew a strong affection and respect.

St Ives became a TRIP opportunity once the branch line was opened on 1 June 1877. It grew to become a firm and lasting favourite for many Swindonian Trippers. Records show that in 1921 over 300 Trippers journeyed to St Ives. In 1924 there were 955 and in 1934, 1,196. It was one of the destinations that was served by a 'night' train. The train would leave Swindon at around 10 p.m. on Thursday or Friday night. It would travel non-stop to Newton Abbott where would it would make a lengthy stop for toilet and refreshment reasons. Later, with toilet facilities onboard this stop became unnecessary. Eventually, after a seven-hour journey, it would arrive in the early hours the following morning.

Normally, mainline trains ran on to Penzance and those wishing to go to St Ives would change at St Erth but, as St Ives man Captain Philip Moran remembers, the TRIP Special Trains would go all the way up to St Ives, although they would have a change of engine. They would be met at St Erth by a couple of 4400s or 2-6-2Ts which would take

Left: Generations of Trippers. Here are granny Win Sparks and granddaughter Susan Murgatroyd, a fourth generation Tripper, paddling in Paignton in 1949. The beach is busy with Swindon Trippers.

Below: The Glass family and friends group in front of beach hut. From left to right, back row: Ron Glass; Dot, his wife; Mrs Rudduck; Mrs Goldsmith and Mr Goldsmith; and Mr Glass Senior, fitter in AM Shop. Front row: Joan (Mary Starley's friend); Mr George Rudduck, seated; Mrs Hilda Glass and the two little Goldsmith girls. This group of friends used to hire the same run of beach huts, Nos 1–5, on Preston Sands, Paignton, every year for many years. At this time (1950s) the weekly rent was about 10s (50p new money) a week.

Arriving at the crack of dawn off the overnight train to St Ives. From left to right: 'Insiders' Mrs Margaret Mudge, and Joy Page, who both worked in the offices, and Colin Page, fitter, erector and turner, pose on Porthmeor Beach at 5.30 a.m. in 1963, the 125th TRIP.

BRITISH RAILWAYS (Western Region)   **THREE**

SWINDON WORKS ANNUAL HOLIDAY, 1962

West of England Trains

SPECIAL TRAINS WILL RUN AS SHOWN BELOW:—

Starting from the

		Station Down Line Platform Friday, July 6th		Rodbourne Lane Sidings Entrance, Park Lane Saturday, July 7th	
		Platform 4	Platform 4		
		Train No. 1	2	5	10
		P.M.	P.M.	A.M.	A.M.
SWINDON	dep.	10.00	10.55	6.00	7.42
Wootton Bassett	,,	—	6.12	—	7.54
Taunton	arr.	—	—	—	9.38
Exeter	,,	—	—	—	10.28
Dawlish Warren	,,	—	—	—	10.49
Dawlish	,,	—	—	—	10.54
Teignmouth	,,	—	—	—	11.02
Newton Abbot	,,	—	—	—	11.12
TORQUAY	,,	—	—	—	11.32
PAIGNTON	,,	—	9.50	—	—
Liskeard	arr.	—	—	4.50 a.m.	—
Bodmin Road	,,	—	—	5.06	—
Lostwithiel	,,	—	—	5.13	—
Par	,,	—	—	5.23	—
St. Austell	,,	—	—	5.36	—
Truro	,,	3.47 a.m.	—	5.58	—
Truro	dep.	5.00	—	—	—
St. Agnes	arr.	5.20	—	—	—
Perranporth	,,	5.36	—	—	—
NEWQUAY	,,	6.12	—	—	—
Redruth	,,	—	—	6.22	—
Gwinear Rd.	,,	—	—	6.33	—
Hayle	,,	—	—	6.40	—
St. Erth	,,	—	—	6.46	—
Marazion	,,	—	—	6.54	—
ST. IVES	,,	4.55	—	—	—
PENZANCE	,,	—	—	7.04	—

On Friday night, July 6th

Passengers for PERRANPORTH and NEWQUAY travel by Train No. 1 in NEWQUAY portion. (Rear of Train)

Passengers for LOOE, travel by Train No. 2, change Liskeard proceeding at 5.55 a.m.

Passengers for WADEBRIDGE and PADSTOW travel by Train No. 2, change Bodmin Road, proceeding at 7.50 a.m.

Passengers for FALMOUTH travel by Train No. 2, change Truro, proceeding at 6.43 a.m.

Passengers for ST. AUSTELL, TRURO and PENZANCE must travel by Train No. 2.

On Saturday, July 7th, passengers for PAIGNTON travel by Train No. 5 only.

Passengers for GOODRINGTON SANDS, CHURSTON, BRIXHAM (change at Churston), KINGSWEAR and DARTMOUTH travel by Train No. 10 and proceed from Torquay by ordinary train at 12.19 p.m.

Passengers for Minehead Line travel by Train No. 10 and change at Taunton.

Passengers travel on Train No. 10 and change at EXETER for:—
EXMOUTH and proceed at 11.15 a.m. from Exeter Central.
BUDE and proceed at 12.02 p.m. from Exeter St. David's.
SEATON and proceed at 11.45 a.m. from Exeter St. David's.
BARNSTAPLE, ILFRACOMBE and BIDEFORD and proceed at 11.34 a.m. from Exeter St. David's.

Note.—The three rear coaches of Train No. 10 will be detached at Newton Abbot.

Passengers for PLYMOUTH, DEVONPORT and LAUNCESTON ONLY travel by 7.05 a.m. ordinary train from Swindon, Saturday, July 7th, due Plymouth N. Rd. 11.35 a.m.

Passengers for WESTON SUPER-MARE travel by ordinary services.

On Sunday to Friday, July 8th to July 20th inclusive, passengers may travel on ordinary services.

RETURN ARRANGEMENTS.

Passengers must return as shown below; those from intermediate or branch line stations must connect with the train at the nearest point.

		Saturday July 14th		Saturday July 21st	
Train No.		29	30	39	37
		P.M.	P.M.	P.M.	P.M.
PENZANCE	dep.	—	2.25	—	2.25
ST. IVES	,,	—	1.56	—	1.56
Marazion	,,	—	2.31	—	—
St. Erth	,,	—	2.48	—	2.45
Hayle	,,	—	—	—	2.50
Gwinear Rd.	,,	—	—	—	3.01
Truro	,,	—	3.33	—	3.33
St. Austell	,,	—	3.58	—	3.58
NEWQUAY	,,	—	2.30	—	2.30
St. Columb Rd.	,,	—	—	—	—
Roche	,,	—	—	—	—
Par	,,	—	4.16	—	4.16
Bodmin Road	,,	—	4.32	—	4.32
Liskeard	,,	—	4.50	—	4.50
Plymouth N. Rd.	,,	—	5.31	—	5.31
PAIGNTON	,,	5.40	—	5.40	—
Torquay	,,	5.50	—	5.50	—
Newton Abbot	,,	6.10	—	6.10	—
Teignmouth	,,	6.20	—	6.20	—
Dawlish	,,	6.28	—	6.28	—
Dawlish Warren	,,	6.35	—	6.35	—
Exeter	,,	—	7.14	—	7.14
Taunton	,,	—	8.05	—	8.05
SWINDON	arr.	9.40	10.03	9.40	10.03

On Saturdays, July 14th and 21st—

Passengers from ST. IVES will depart 1.56 p.m. and travel on through coaches to Swindon.

Passengers from FALMOUTH depart 2.05 p.m. and join Specials No. 30 or 37 at Truro.

Passengers from NEWQUAY depart 2.30 p.m. and travel on through coaches to Swindon. PERRANPORTH passengers depart 1.55 p.m. and travel in Special from TRURO.

Passengers from PADSTOW depart 3.13 p.m. and WADEBRIDGE 3.24 p.m. connecting with Trains No. 30 and 37 at Bodmin Road.

Passengers from LOOE depart 3.50 p.m. connect with Trains No. 30 and 37 at Liskeard.

Passengers from DEVONPORT, PLYMOUTH and LAUNCESTON must travel on Special Trains shown above.

Passengers from KINGSBRIDGE depart 4.35 p.m. by ordinary train, change at Brent and join Specials at Newton Abbot.

Passengers from BUDE depart 3.09 p.m. (change Okehampton) and join Special at Exeter.

Passengers from SIDMOUTH depart 4.30 p.m. and SEATON depart 4.27 p.m. Change at Exeter Central, joining Special Train at Exeter St. David's.

Passengers from EXMOUTH depart 5.15 p.m. change at Exeter Central, joining Special Train at Exeter St. David's.

Passengers from BIDEFORD depart 2.56 p.m. change at Barnstaple Jct., connect 3.50 p.m., arriving Taunton 5.48 p.m. and join Special.

Passengers from ILFRACOMBE and MORTEHOE travel on 2.55 p.m. ex Ilfracombe, arrive Taunton 5.48 p.m. and join Special.

Passengers from MINEHEAD depart 6.40 p.m. and connect with Special at Taunton.

Passengers from DARTMOUTH, KINGSWEAR, BRIXHAM, CHURSTON and GOODRINGTON SANDS travel by the 4.10 ordinary train ex Kingswear changing to Special Train at Paignton.

On any day, Sunday to Friday, passengers return by any ordinary services.

Chief Mech. and Elec. Engr's Dept.,
Swindon.
June, 1962.

R. A. SMEDDLE

PRINTED BY THE BOROUGH PRESS (SWINDON) LTD., EASTCOTT HILL, SWINDON

From this train's schedule we can deduce a great deal. Only four TRIP Specials are laid on for this whole region. Much more use is made of the ordinary train service. Weston-super-Mare, once the second most popular choice, now does not warrant even one Special Train.

it over the little single-track branch line and all the way into the station itself. Returning trains would also run right through from St Ives to Swindon. This was still happening as late as 1962.

In 1931 the No.1 St Ives Special was made up of ten Thirds and two Brake Thirds and departed Thursday night. In 1953 the No.1 St Ives Special, formation Brake Third, seven Thirds and Brake Third (270 tons), departed on Friday night. Captain Moran remembers that the trains would be split in two and a half at a time would be pulled into the station to accommodate disembarkation. The Trippers would alight at 5 a.m. The locals would be waiting on the Malakoff, a promontory overlooking the town and station, to meet and greet the Swindoners. Mrs. Joyce Murgatroyd remembers that the landladies would call out their own names and those of the people who had booked with them. They would then escort them to their lodgings, helping with the luggage or little children. 'It is just as well they did', she said, 'because we had no idea at all where the cottages were and would never have found them in the dark.' The townspeople would gather again to see them off when they left for home and Tom Richards, author and previous St Ives resident, remembers as a small lad being taken to wave the Swindoners goodbye. It was this warm welcome and fond farewell that many Swindonians remember. A Mr H. Bickham of Newhall Street, wrote to the *St. Ives Times* in 1936 to express appreciation of this. He said:

> May I... express on behalf of Swindonians our appreciation of the kindly and spontaneous welcome extended by the inhabitants of St Ives. This very friendly gesture on the occasion of our annual holiday, very much enhances the pleasure afforded in a visit to your delightful resort.

Mrs Ivy Lawrence, who had worked as a ward orderly in the GWR hospital in the railway village, had warm, happy memories of St Ives and the welcome they got. Ivy and her extended family returned again and again to St Ives, drawn by its beauty and quietness, but mostly by the warm reception the Trippers received from their hosts.

> We went down there from when I was little... year after year we went... we knew all St Ives, and really all the people. Mind you it was full of Swindon people. St Ives called it 'Swindon Week'. All our family went and then my family's family went... my brother and his little boy used to go and of course Grampy when he was alive. There was not a lot going on, but it was pretty and Swindon people loved going there.
>
> The platform would be packed when we got there. The people at St Ives would come and meet everyone at the station. Didn't matter what the time was, they used to meet us and kiss us and they helped you carry your stuff. They would come and see us all off again at the end and oh then there would be tears and kisses. Some people stayed with the same people each year so they got very friendly see. The landladies would be standing there crying their eyes out... really!
>
> Oh it was lovely there, quiet like but nice. We used to go down on the beach every day and hire a hut. We'd sit in the deckchairs like and mother used to butter split rolls and we'd have a tray of tea.

Ivy remembered another tradition that strengthened the bonds between Swindon and St Ives. She particularly remembered that the young men of Swindon Works used to go to St Ives with high hopes of finding their future wives. She recalled that Swindon railway families often used to say, 'go on TRIP to St Ives and come back with a bride!'

Swindon young men from the Works got their wives at St Ives. It was known that when they went down on Trip Week they'd look to get to know a girl like, and then they used to go down at Christmas, to carry on the courting!

If all went well, the next TRIP would be for wedding bells. The new bride would then accompany her husband on the return TRIP Special to her new life in Swindon.

Mrs Jean Spicer went to St Ives for several years in the 1930s with her father, Mr Sidney Dickson, a carriage finisher who worked in 7 Shop, her mother and brother Ernest. She remembers the lodgings they stayed in:

It was a fisherman's cottage right close to the beach. There was a great flight of steps to get up into the house, and underneath was where her husband kept the boat which went out through the doors onto the beach. It wasn't the most popular beach where they were, but it was good to walk all along there.

The Cockbill family also spent many holidays at St Ives, staying, at different times, in Fish Street, Cancrows Street, Teetotal Street, The Warren, Barnoon Terrrace and Upper Ayr, the latter an experience their father would not repeat whilst still having youngsters in a pushchair as it was a long walk down and a steep push back up! Brian fondly remembers many of the family's special TRIP rituals – fish and chips from Berryman's chippy in Fore Street, the extravagance of bright yellow ice creams made from thick Cornish cream (although this was not available on Sundays), weighing themselves at the beginning and end of each holiday on the machine at the harbour front, and playing the Minstrel Band machine in the amusement arcade which belted out 'American Patrol'. Trevor recalled the St Ives' special GWR connection:

My parents usually favoured St Ives, they had tried other places but found nothing to compare with The Warren and Porthminster beach where one could paddle in safety and dig sand-castles and , best of all, watch little Swindon-made tank engines (45XX class) pull Swindon-built coaches (chocolate and cream) into and out of the station.

Captain Philip Moran remembers that St Ives people were happy to accommodate the Swindoners as best they could. Knowing that the visitors were on very limited budgets, they even, at times, put the Trippers up in drill halls. Philip distinctly remembers the long queues of Trippers early each morning outside the Blue Haven Café waiting to get in for a hearty breakfast. He also remembers the long queues of men and boys waiting to go on a fishing trip. Captain Moran believes that Swindon TRIP holiday probably laid the foundations for the St Ives tourist industry.

The bonds of affection between the railway people of Swindon and the people of St Ives were real, strong and long lasting but not always without hiccups. Brian Cockbill recalls that there were times when the 'rowdies' amongst the Trippers caused a high degree of consternation in St Ives residents. Adverse letters in the local press even threatened to boycott future bookings for Swindon railway families. There were, however, many things that gave mutual pleasure and mutual respect. The annual cricket match between the local club and an ad hoc Tripper team put together on the train journey down, usually played at the recreation ground, was a tradition that has stayed in Swindonian memories. It was one of the TRIP highlights that both sides looked forward to as 'Offstump' acknowledged in the *Western Echo* (St Ives). He writes in 1936 that, 'much interest was evinced in the annual game with the Swindon holiday makers at the Recreation Ground on Wednesday evening'. It was not a good contest for the visitors as the score card shows.

An elegant study of man and dog and white daps. Fred Sparks, carpenter, and Nell pose on St Ives beach in 1925. Fred always liked to be well turned out for TRIP as the family photo album shows.

Cricket Match
Swindon

1936
St Ives

E. Painter, b Cocking, 3.
M. Telling, b Pitman, 11.
S. King, c C Walker, b Williams, 1.
M. Uren, c Williams, b Pitman, 1.
G. Walker, b Dunstan, 4.
L. Griggs, c Cocks, b Firth, 0.
R. Clack, c White, b Firth, 13.
S, Uren, c and b Williams, 0.
J. Voulls, b Williams, 0.
T, Paynter, c . Walker, b Firth, 10.
L. Harris, b Firth, 0.
G. Nicholls, not out, 0.
Extras 0. Total 43.

T. Firth, b Uren, 10.
H. Dunstan, b Uren 0.
S. Scoble, b Uren 0.
S. Freeman, b Glack, 6.
U. Cocking, c Ricks, b Nicholls 7.
S. Cock, runout, 11.
J. Walker lbw, b Uren 4.
C. Walker, st Telling, b Uren 11.
T. Adams, b Nicholls, 31.
W.H. Williams not out 13.
C. Pitman, c Nicholls, b Voulls 0.
K. White, b Voulls, 0.
Extras 4. Total 97.

St Ives took the match scoring 97 runs and the Swindoners managed just 43! It was good that young Ron Clack's dad had rescued him from the trackside in his early years, as it would appear that Ron, now aged sixteen, was 'Man of the Match' for Swindon, although not up to the scoring of St Ives' T. Adams. The St Ives Cricket Club and the St Ives Carnival Committee would take up a collection which would be donated to the Swindon's Poor Kiddies Outing Fund. On this occasion it was £1 6s 7½d. This generosity of spirit was reciprocated by the Swindonians. In 1939, whilst out on a rescue mission, the St Ives's lifeboat capsized many times. Seven of the

Brian Cockbill vividly remembers that every year without fail the lifeboat was launched during TRIP at St Ives. Whether it was for a practice session or for a rescue mission it always generated great interest. Here, in 1934, there would have been many Trippers amongst these onlookers.

eight lifeboat men lost their lives. The terrible tragedy was deeply felt in Swindon. Those 'Inside' Swindon Works organised a special collection for the dependants of the lost men.

Joyce Murgatroyd recalls of the 1920s and '30s that St Ives people put on a number of events to make the Trippers feel welcome. On many evenings locals would gather in the harbour and sing as a choir. On Sunday evenings she remembers open-air Church Services on Smeaton's Pier. In later decades Brian Cockbill remembers that the Salvation Army would conduct a Sunday Service at the slipway near the Sloop. The most memorable event for Joyce was, however, the 'soot and flour fight', when teams of men in boats would pelt teams of men in other boats with bags of flour and soot. 'You never saw such a mess in your life', she says laughingly. 'Afterwards they would all dive into the water to wash it off. Great fun.'

Undoubtedly, St Ives holds a special place in the memories of Swindon Trippers and Swindon TRIP has a special place in the history of St Ives.

PENZANCE

Penzance, lying in the sheltered curve of Mount's Bay, only really became a resort when the railway arrived there in the second half of the nineteenth century. With its beaches around every corner and numerous coves to explore, it soon became a firm favourite with holidaymakers and with Trippers. Numbers choosing Penzance in 1931 totalled 692, made up of 540 adults with 152 children.

Mr Charlie Gee was born in 1911, the eighth child in a family of nine boys. His father was a clerk in the Works. It would have been incredibly challenging to bring up such a large family on a railway clerk's income. Mr Gee Senior managed to get three of his sons jobs 'Inside': Charlie, a coach finisher, Bert, a boilermaker, and Cecil, a clerk like his father. Charlie remembers that his big family started with just a day out at Weston-super-Mare, taking their sandwiches with them. Later they managed a week at Penzance, although not all of them all the time. Charlie's father loved Penzance. He was especially fond of the fresh fish he could buy there, which he would often take back for the landlady to prepare for their meals. Charlie remembers Penzance for other reasons. Despite being told not to put his head out of the train window, that is what Charlie did, on and off, for most of the seven-hour journey. By the time he got to Penzance he was feeling decidedly poorly. Charlie spent the next three days in bed with a very heavy cold, being looked after by the kindly landlady, whilst his family were out and about enjoying themselves. By the time he was up, half his holiday had gone!

TENBY

An early 1900s advertising postcard describes Tenby as having, 'a mild and salubrious climate, picturesque scenery, unrivalled sea bathing, good fishing and boating and fine golf links. Not only that, Tenby stands on a headland above two fine sandy beaches, North Beach and South Beach'.

In 1892, 310 Swindon Trippers holidayed in Tenby. In 1934, 582 went there. In 1953, it was still popular with 202. Compared to other TRIP destinations the numbers were not large, but the impact on Tenby and its inhabitants was massive. Tenby was used to numbers of visitors arriving by train for Works' Week, but it developed a special relationship with those from Swindon Works.

A splendid set of gentlemen - the staff of the Great Western's Tenby Station, arranged on the down platform in 1906. The Station Master, Mr James Bowen, would have overseen TRIP arrivals and departures. The gentleman sporting the straw-boater tucked in on the end looks like a Swindon Tripper just arrived for his holiday. (Ken Daniels. Mr Daniel's father worked for the GWR in the Saundersfoot signal box)

Above: This throng of people features Tenbyites and Swindon Trippers on the North Beach after the beach sports in 1911. The message on the back says, '*This is the Swindon GWR sports on the beach*'. They all look remarkably over-dressed for sports activities, presumably they were the supporters. (Ken Daniels)

Right: Twenty-seven years after 1911, Lorna Dawes remembers the excitement of Sports Day on Tenby North Beach in 1938 and the crowds that gathered to watch them.

The three-legged race, the wheelbarrow and the sack race were a regular feature in the TRIP sports events at Tenby and were as popular in 1938 as in 1924 when reported on in the *Evening Advertiser* newspaper.

Mr Ivor Jenkins, who grew up in Tenby, believes this was because Tenby people had great respect for railwaymen, especially GWR railwaymen. They admired the quality of them and stood in awe of their well-earned reputation as fine tradesmen. Tenby also boasted a fine GWR station and splendid station staff.

Mr Jenkins remembers as a young lad in the 1930s looking forward to Swindon Week with great anticipation of the fun and pleasure to come. He says:

> I learned that Swindoners were wonderful people. During their stay they became part of Tenby, true 'locals' and took part in all the local activities. They had their own children with them and made sure there were enough activities and events organised (mainly on the beach) to keep them occupied and interested. As far as the Swindoners were concerned, we, the Tenby children, were automatically part of their 'family' and could join in at any time.

Mr Jones holds these memories in such affection that he sends a special thanks to those Swindon Trippers, 'for helping me to have a wonderful childhood'. It was, by all accounts, a favour returned. The Tenby people helped the Swindon children to have 'a wonderful childhood' too, or, at least a great summer holiday if 1924 is anything to go by!

1924 was the record-breaking year of all time for TRIP. That year 29,000 went away, several hundred of whom went to Tenby. The local Tradesmen's Association, together with the local branch of the British Legion, laid on a splendid array of amusements over the week. Monday had 'fighting-the-tide' on South Beach with fifty-six entrants; it was a popular game. On Tuesday they held 'Rustic Sports' on North Hill beach, with events such as three-legged races, barrow races and egg and spoon races, for girls, boys and 'veterans'. On Wednesday there was a Fancy Dress Carnival with lots of prize-winning categories, which was followed by 'variety entertainment' in the evening. Lastly, there was a whist drive and dance with yet more chances of winning prizes.

Right: Lorna Dawes' family lodged with Mrs Rees at 1a Greenhill Road, Tenby for many years, and Lorna, her brother Kenneth and Dorothy Rees became good friends.

Below: The Dickson family at Exmouth. From left to right: Mrs Elizabeth Dickson and her son Ernest, aged six years, Mr Sidney Dickson, a carriage finisher and his daughter Jean, aged about eight years. Jean remembers that the water ring was a necessary piece of their holiday equipment as Ernest was not good at swimming. Jean loved swimming and believes that Swindon youngsters were usually very good swimmers as they had free lessons at Milton Road Baths in the town centre.

It was a truly memorable time and one that was repeated over many decades. Miss Lorna Dawes recalls the excitement of sitting on North Sands as a little girl, watching the men's wheelbarrow and three-legged races, children's sack races and the women's sprint race in the late 1930s.

Lorna's dad, Albert Edward, the third eldest in a family of eight, was a cylinder moulder in the Iron Foundry. His father, Albert Ernest, worked in the Rolling Mills at the turn of the twentieth century. Lorna went 'Inside' as office messenger girl in 1945, eventually working in many of the Works' offices during her forty-plus years of service. One of her roles was helping to make TRIP happen by working overtime in the Works Booking Office issuing Priv tickets. Lorna's family returned again and again to Tenby staying at 1a Greenhill Road, two big cottages joined together with a lovely large garden. In later years Lorna would book one of the railway coaches parked up alongside Tenby Station for the family to stay in. It was, she remembers, big and comfortable, but lacking in mod cons, that is to say no water and no loos! One had to collect one's water from the taps, and empty one's potty in the station's toilets.

Mrs Jean Spicer also recalls the fun times her family had at Tenby. Jean's father, Sidney Dickson, was a third-generation railwayman who worked as a carriage finisher or what was latterly known as a coach finisher. Funnily, Jean remembers not the usual building of sandcastles, but more the excitement of watching them being knocked down!

> I remember at Tenby in about 1938. On Wednesday when it was early closing day, the trades people used to come and give prizes. They issued everyone with a little Union Jack. You had about four children to a sandcastle which were all in a line. You patted down your sandcastle as hard as you could, It all depended on the timing of when the tide was coming in. The last sandcastle to fall got the first prize. As they would fall, we got a prize. Some of them were sweets, some were old stock I think. Some them were quite useful ones, some not very good for children, but it was nice.

No wonder Swindonians and Tenbyites remember Swindon Week so well.

EXMOUTH

Exmouth was another firm favourite with Swindon Trippers, especially with the Spicer family. Jean says, 'We liked Exmouth. You see more of the water. It is in more – more than at Weston, St Ives and Tenby.' That was important to Jean as she liked swimming.

In 1931 Special No.14, made up of twelve Thirds and two Brake Thirds, left Rodborne Lane sidings at 5.15 a.m. carrying 505 adults and 213 children for Exmouth. In 1953 overall numbers had significantly decreased. That year the No.14 Special, made up of seven Thirds and two Brake Thirds, left Rodborne Lane Sidings at 7.55 a.m. carrying 182 adults and eighty-five children, destination Exmouth. In 1961 the No.14 Special to Exmouth was still departing from Rodborne Lane Sidings at 7.55 a.m. The formation, however, differed in that it was made up of six Seconds and two Brake Compos. This train carried 340 passengers, 213 for Taunton, twenty-seven for disembarkation at Exeter, and only 100 going on to Exmouth.

These were a handful of the much-loved destinations visited by Swindon Trippers. They give us a flavour of TRIP, but we must remember that TRIP was not confined to the South West and Wales. London, Birmingham, Chester, Yarmouth and Manchester, to name a very few, had their fair share of regular Trippers, too. TRIP eventually went all over the country and even abroad. To write about all of the destinations would require a book of its own.

— CHAPTER FOUR —
IMPORTANT FACTS AND SIGNIFICANT YEARS

1848: First TRIP to Oxford.

1849: TRI[to Torquay.

1868: For the first time three Special TRIP Trains are run: one to London, one to Weston-super-Mare and one to South Wales.[1]

1869: TRIP has grown into a five-day break.

1874: TRIP holiday had now grown into a nine-day break.

1892: It is reported that Swindon Works is now the largest railway factory in the world. 18,248 go on TRIP this year. By this time there were several destinations but Weymouth and Weston-super-Mare had well and truly established themselves as the most popular.

1889
Great Western Magazine and Temperance Union Record

Swindon Mechanics' Annual Trip

Destination	Adults	Children	Total
London	1,870	1,289	3,159
West of England	2,657	2,088	4,745
Weymouth	1,874	1,747	3,621
South Wales	1,560	1.210	2,770
North of England	1,439	951	2,390
Total	9,400	7,285	16,685

This figure is an increase of 2,123 over the previous year.

1896 is a milestone year in that for the first time special trains are laid on for the return journey as well as for the outward journey. Up until this time it was the practice for the Trippers to return by ordinary trains during the following week. The Mechanics' Institution Annual Report duly records its thanks to the directors of the company for this extended special service. Also, it is instructed for the first time, by G.J. Churchward, that, 'arrangements will be made for compartments to be set apart for the use of Foremen, Clerks etc.' on the Special TRIP Trains. This would have been a welcome touch of comfort and distinction and would have been seen as an 'extra perk' of rank.

TRIP 1892

POPULATION 36000
TRAVELLING 18248
50·7% OF POP^N.

LONDON AREA	2832	WEST	3778
S.WALES	2959	NORTH	2193
WEYMOUTH	4524	WESTON	1972

SOME OTHER DESTINATIONS -

TEIGNMOUTH 642   PENZANCE 81   TORQUAY 172

FALMOUTH 14   NEWQUAY 7   TENBY 310

WINCHESTER 147   PLYMOUTH 586   CLEVEDON 54

N.ABBOT 1583   MINEHEAD 37   BIRMINGHAM 400

MANCHESTER 360   CHESTER 493   BIRK'HEAD 555

BOURNEMOUTH 4   EXMOUTH 1

One of a prepared series of summaries of information relating to TRIP. Note the population growth in the town and the percentage that go away on TRIP. In 1851 the town had a population of 4,879, divided almost equally between old and new town. Just half a century later in 1901, that had increased to over 40,000!

G.W.R.
"The Record Trip".
Over
22,000
of us
went
in one day!

A record-breaking year for TRIP. It was to be the first among many record-breaking years.

1900

This was the first year recorded as 'The Record Trip'. It was, in fact, the first of many 'records' as TRIP continued to grow. An article in *The Railway Magazine*, a well-respected publication of the time, describes the event as, 'unique in railway annals both in time and traffic records'. It informs its readers:

> On the chosen day of July 1900, no less than 22,500 people of all ranks, sizes and conditions connected with the Great Western Railway… set forth on their annual trips.

It is greatly impressed by the fact, that whilst other companies may convey large numbers of their employees to 'one selected town', the GWR believes, 'it best consults the wishes and desires of so many varied minds and interests by letting the workers have a wide choice'. It is amazed by the fact that the twenty Special Trains and two ordinaries, amounting to 392 coaches, required to convey this 'tremendous burden' were all dispatched between 4.55 a.m. and 6.40 a.m., 'the most incredible time of 1 hour 45 minutes', and all done without interfering with the ordinary traffic of the GWR at Swindon or elsewhere, 'even in the smallest degree', despite the heavy fog that shrouded the area. It sings the praises of the Great Western Railway, saying, 'it is wonderful in many ways, not least in this annual trip'.

1902

By this time the GWR's in-house magazine had undergone a number of changes and had become simply the *Great Western Railway Magazine*. It reports in detail on the 'annual TRIP' with particular reference as to how TRIP traffic was worked. From the details given it is clear that this aspect of TRIP working changed little over the following decades.

There were five different points of embarkation:

Up mainline platform	London and Winchester
Down South Wales platform	Swansea, Pembroke and New Milford
Carriage sidings	Weymouth
Sawmill sidings	Plymouth, Penzance, Newton Abbott and Weston-super-Mare
Locomotive yard	Birkenhead and Manchester

There were over 21,000 passengers to be got away on twenty-one trains. The first departed at 4.55 a.m., the last just two hours later at 6.55 a.m. That is one train departure every 5.71 minutes! This is even more impressive when one remembers that the block system, or space interval working, was in practice then whereby every in-between block had to be train free, i.e. a train could not enter the block in front, until the train ahead had left it. The trains would have been belled on from signal box to signal box and any problems belled back with instructions for the train behind. Taking into account the fact that it would take a steam engine four to five minutes to make headway, this was a superb piece of operation at maximum capacity. The article's comment, 'a brilliant achievement!', seems to be something of an understatement. All this was accomplished by bringing in extra staff of high calibre to help the existing staff. Mr Brewer of Swindon Station was ably assisted by Chief Station Inspector Rochester, Chief Yard Inspector Ball, Inspectors Simpkins and Spurlock and Acting Inspector A. Rochester. Chief Divisional Inspector Forrister (Bristol) and District Inspector (Chippenham) were also present. The locomotive arrangements were superintended by Mr W.H. Waister's staff and Superintendent Johnson (Paddington).

1903
Great Western Railway Magazine

Destination	Adults	Children	Total
London	2,246	1,359	3,605
West of England	3,033	1,928	4,961
Weston-Super-Mare	1,541	1,619	3,160
Weymouth	2,747	2,555	5,302
South Wales	1,838	1,372	3,210
North of England	1,583	764	2,347
Total 1903	12,988	9,597	22,585
Increase	931	407	1,338

1905

Getting to the trains so early in the morning meant, for most of the Trippers, walking or taking the tram as very few railwaymen could afford taxis. On 3 July a resolution was put to the Electricity and Tramways Committee that for the Special TRIP trams running from 3.30 a.m. to 6 a.m. on Friday 7 July, the fare be 1*d* a stage, not the usual 1/2*d*. Councillor Walters was most unhappy at this proposal and requested for an amendment. TRIP morning was, he told the Committee, the 'people's day', and he called on the Corporation to 'do its duty to the people' who had been so supportive of the tramway undertaking. He was unsuccessful and so the Trippers who took the tram had to pay more for their ride.

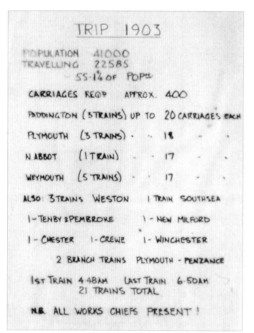

What is staggering to see here is that over half the population, 55.1 per cent of the town, leave on TRIP. How empty it must have felt. A proverbial Ghost Town. No wonder shopkeepers closed or drastically reduced their stocks or dropped their prices to bring customers in.

1906

The *Great Western Railway Magazine* reports that a new destination has been added to the possibilities for TRIP – 'Aberystwyth a beautiful watering place on the West Coast of Wales'. This was made possible by the takeover by the GWR of the Manchester & Milford Railway on 1 July of this year. Such was the interest in this new destination that a large number including Mr and Mrs W.H. Williams, the Mayor and Mayoress of Swindon, chose to go there. Aberystwyth proved a popular choice from then on.

1908
Great Western Railway Magazine

Destinations	Adults	Children	Total	Difference over 1907	
				Inc.	Dec.
London	2,870	1,498	4,368	146	–
West of England	3,192	1,792	4,984	–	509
Weston-super-Mare	2,142	2,055	4,197	–	288
Weymouth	3,121	3,050	6,171	392	–
South Wales	1,660	1,110	2,770	–	284
North of England	1,434	640	2,074	–	432
Total 1908 Total 1907	14,419 15,035	10,145 10,504	24,564 25,539		
Decrease	616	359	975		

1910
Great Western Railway Magazine

Destination	Adults	Children	Total
London	2,541	1,332	3,873
West of England	3,025	1,912	4,937
Weston-super-Mare	2,165	2,029	4,194
Weymouth	2,949	2,915	5,864
South Wales	1,662	1,142	2,804
North of England	1,251	611	1,862
Total 1910	13,593	9,941	23,534
Decrease	425	162	587

1911

Every year those reporting on TRIP proudly proclaimed that 'everything passed off as smoothly as possible' or 'the trains were got away without incident'. In 1911 there was an incident! It was not reported on until the following year's *Evening Advertiser's* write-up on TRIP. An 'accidence of small importance' occurred when local footballer Woolford, 'slightly injured his knee in attempting to board a train'. The article informs us that there has never been an accident of a serious nature 'since the annual TRIP was instituted'. It was an extraordinary record considering the hundreds of thousands that had gone off on TRIP Trains.

1912

At first glance 1912 looks little different than the TRIP of previous years. There was all the usual excitement, the same preparations, people put in their usual requests and workers and their families went to all the usual places, but there was one significant difference that was to set a new trend and become standard practice for many years.

Night Trains

For the very first time trains were run to the West Country the night before the usual holiday start. The management of TRIP had always been a wizardry of magic formulas to get the thousands of trippers to their destinations, but now the sheer numbers of men, women and children who wanted to 'go West', well over 10,000, meant that the timescale to work the magic had to be expanded to enable them and all the other trippers to be got away during the next morning. So it was on Thursday evening, 11 July 1912, that the first two night trains were dispatched for destinations in the West Country at 10.40 and 10.55 p.m. from the down platform at Swindon Junction Station.

The *Great Western Railway Magazine* announced it:

> For the first time in the history of the trip the West of England working, which is amongst the heaviest, was appreciably relieved by the running of two special trains the night before. The trains were each formed of 14 vehicles and the fact that they were heavily laden is proof that the concession met with its object.

The first of these 'historic' trains was hauled by a 'Star' class No.4011 *Knight of the Garter* driven by driver Knapman, and fifteen minutes later driver Moore took out another 'Star', No.4015 *Knight of St John*. As was stated, these West Country trains consisted of fourteen coaches and both ran from Swindon to Chippenham, on through Trowbridge and Westbury to Taunton. Stops were scheduled at Newton Abbott to allow use of the toilet facilities. Thereafter, from Par the trains stopped at the junction stations serving the popular holiday destinations. The first train arrived in Penzance eight hours later at 6.20 a.m., at which time there were still four more West Country trains yet to leave Swindon. In all, 902 adults and 371 children disembarked at Penzance. Some, those who had not made any lodging bookings, obviously had a very early beach start to their holidays. These trains were not sleepers and the trippers were obliged to sit up throughout the journey, although possibly allowing the children to sleep in the luggage racks. What these 'pioneering' travellers thought of these new arrangements one would love to know.

On the following morning it was business as usual. Despite the new overnight relief three more trains consisting of fourteen and fifteen coaches were necessary for the West of England

and they departed from Rodbourne Lane sidings. The first two of these, the 5.05 a.m. and the 5.20 a.m. went only as far as Plymouth via a rather circuitous route of Bristol (Temple Meads) via the Badminton line and on to Plymouth. The later 6.05 a.m. West Country train left from the sawmills for Kingswear hauled by No.181 *Ivanhoe*. The *Ivanhoe* had undergone a rebuild from a 4-4-2 to a 4-6-0 during the months of March to July, and this was probably one of her first trips 'in traffic' in her new guise.

The actual first train away in the morning was the heavily laden fourteen-coach 4.55 a.m. departure for Weymouth hauled by a 4-4-0 No.3728, an un-named member of the 'Bulldog' class, with four others equally heavily laden following behind up until 6.20 a.m. The last of these was the oldest engine in this group, namely the 'Barnum' 2-4-0 No.3210, built in 1889. Weymouth passengers had to make their way to part of the Carriage Work Sidings south of the main line as did those whose destinations was the ever popular Weston. These lucky passengers, because of the short duration of the journey at just under two hours, had the luxury of comparatively 'late' departures between 6.30 and 7.0 a.m.

For those wishing to go via London, three trains of fifteen coaches each were run up to Paddington, all hauled by 4-6-0 'Saint' class locomotives. Two trains delivered passengers to the North and one twelve-coach special to the South of England. This was worked by an elderly 1868 0-6-0 'Standard Goods' No.430 engine which had only then been recently fitted with a B4 boiler and which definitely needed the tender loving care of an experienced driver. The bulk of trippers had been sent on their way and another TRIP, a landmark in its history, that was destined to be a trendsetter, had been successfully accomplished.

1913
Great Western Railway Magazine

Destination	Adults	Children	Total	Difference over 1912	
				Inc.	Dec.
London	2,406	1,261	3,667	–	224
West of England	3,779	2,271	6,050	–	220
Weston-super-Mare	2,429	2,225	4,654	91	–
Weymouth	2,860	2,650	5,510	–	1,052
South Wales	1,811	1,201	3,012	357	–
North of England	1,314	638	1,952	69	–
Total 1913 Total 1912	14,599 15,135	10,246 10,689	24,845 25,824		
Decrease	536	443	979		

1913

On Thursday 22 May 1913, the *Swindon Advertiser* carried a significant item of news not only for the employees at the Works and their families, but for all the inhabitants of Swindon town. It stated that there was to be a rearrangement of TRIP. Prior to this it had been the practice for the Works to close down on the Thursday evening and reopen on Monday week. The previous year, 1912, was the first time Special TRIP Trains had run from Thursday evening followed by the main exodus on Friday morning but now this was all to change.

The *Swindon Advertiser* had a small article giving details of the reasons behind this decision. Entitled 'The G.W.R. 'trip' date altered', it explains:

> Friday has hitherto been the day selected for closing the Works and Monday morning that of re-opening. but with the advent of the Insurance Act and the clauses referring to Unemployment, a loss would have occurred to the workmen were they absent during six days in one week as under the old arrangement. The employers in such cases would not have to pay their proportion of the contributions. The officials of the Company, it is presumed, recognised this, and very generously, we consider, and if we are right in our conjecture, gave the men the option of dividing the holidays between two weeks, thus obviating any loss to the workmen, but entailing upon the Company the payment of their share of many thousands of contributions.

The *North Wilts Herald* of the same date confirms that complications would have arisen under the Insurance Act if the old order of events had been maintained, but believes the changes were effected as a result of a, 'canvass amongst the men, the majority of whom voted in favour of a bare week's holiday'. It goes on to report that this year's TRIP will start from 5.30 p.m. on Wednesday 9 July to Thursday 17 July, 'so that the annual holiday will really be curtailed by a couple of days'. This new arrangement required that three Special Trains would leave Swindon on Wednesday 9 July followed by the usual exodus the following morning. Return journeys had to be made no later than Wednesday 16 July.

The Daily Chronicle of Wednesday 21 May is more forthright and a lot more blunt. Under the headlines of:

Swindon holiday curtailed
Two days less than before
'The Grand March Past' avoided

it informs its readers that:

> While the men are away on their 'trip' wages are not being paid to them, so that they are really unemployed and it was the difficulty in relation to this particular phase of the arrangements which has resulted in the shortening of the holiday. The employees, so a 'Daily Chronicle' representative was informed yesterday, have been canvassed regarding the matter, and in consequence of the monetary losses which would accrue, the majority of them have voted for the bare week's holiday, and unemployment benefit will not be claimed. This arrangement really means that the employees cannot now claim unemployment benefit owing to the splitting up of the weeks.

It is interesting to see the different 'interpretations' of the event from the differing political stance of particular newspapers. On the one hand we are led to believe this new arrangement is purely because of the magnanimity of the company to assist all, whilst on the other hand we are left to feel that the men are definitely losing out.

From the company perspective, according to Circular 2276 dated 14 May, written by C.B. Collett, it was viewed as 'a complication' which could lead to a lot of work and a loss of a lot of money. It states:

> It appears that the whole of the men who are insured against unemployment can claim benefit for the last two days of the usual Trip Holiday which, from the Insurance Officers' point of view is undesirable on account of the amount of money which it will be necessary to pay out and the elaborate arrangements that will have to be made to do so.
>
> The Company is also threatened with the loss of the rebate it would otherwise be entitled to by not providing a continuous employment for the year. The matter is under consideration, but in the meantime I shall be glad if you will kindly ascertain the general feeling of the men under your control as to whether a holiday of a week's duration would be as acceptable as the usual 10 days.

Later in Circular 2281 of 21 May, Mr Collett found that:

> … a very large majority of the men prefer to have a holiday of a week's duration instead of 9 days as formally. The most convenient dates are found to be from the middle of one week to the middle of the next and accordingly it has been arranged for the Loco. Works to be close from 5.30pm on Wednesday July 9 until 9.0am Thursday July 17.

This must have come as something of an enormous relief to the company, particularly as the implementation of the Act was costing them in the region of £60,000 a year. What it meant to the men was a longer working year but less time without pay. This new way would mean that the men would go into work on Thursday morning and be able to draw half a week's pay as a result. So, to quote the *Chronicle*, 'the burden of the father with the big family and comparatively small wage will be lightened and he will return to work with a much better heart', even if he did resent the fact that he had lost two work-free days. It is ironic that an Act that was made to protect the interests of workers had an initial effect of making them forfeit work-free days. The nine-day holiday was no longer an option for them. (Incidentally, the ten days in the first circular and the nine days in the second are as written, and *not* a typing error!)

However, these new arrangements would have had a knock-on effect that would adversely affect the economics of the town and the livelihoods of many of the town's shopkeepers. Traditionally, the day before TRIP holiday was one of the busiest commercial days in the whole year for the town. This manic shopping spree helped to make up for the total absence of shoppers in the days during TRIP. It all hinged on the fact that Wednesday was early closing day and the Trippers would be departing first thing Thursday morning. Swindon shops could not afford to lose such vital shopping time. No wonder then that the new proposals rang bells of alarm and that anxious shopkeepers attended a special meeting of the Chamber of Commerce on Tuesday 10 June, to discuss the matter. The matter had already been discussed in committee and referred to the Home Office and at this special meeting the Mayor reported that:

> … that department had replied that the only way by which the difficulty could be surmounted was by the revocation of the existing order under the Shops Act and the making of a new one in which the provision might be made for the opening on the Wednesday before the excursion and closing on the Thursday.

The Mayor went on to explain that this required not only two special meetings of the Council but also the submission of a petition signed by the members of the Chamber asking for such a new order. Needless to say the decision was made to do just that. Notice of this new Weekly Half-Holiday (Amended) Order was duly given and the resolution adopted by the Council was as follows:

> The Mayor, Aldermen and Burgesses of the borough acting by the council in pursuance of the powers conferred upon them by the Shops Act 1912 and after due compliance with its provisions do Hereby order as follows:
> (1)　The Swindon Weekly Half-Holiday (Amended) Order 1913
> made by us on May 6 last is hereby revoked as from July 1, 1913;
> (2)　this order which may be cited as the Swindon Weekly Half-Holiday (Amended) Order 1913 applies to all shops in the borough except... shops exempted by the Act, or by an order made in pursuance of the... Act from the obligation to close for the weekly half holiday.
> All shops to which this order applies shall be closed for the weekly half-holidays on Wednesday at 1 p.m. throughout the year, except on the Wednesday immediately preceding the commencement of the Swindon annual holiday week, otherwise called Trip Week. In the week Trip commences all shops to which this order applies shall be closed on Thursday at 1 p.m.

Thus is illustrated the impact and power of TRIP!

1915

It took an historic event of world-affecting proportion to halt TRIP. Never before had there been anything that had caused even the slightest ripple of disorderliness or hampering of schedules but the First World War brought it to dead halt. The serious state of affairs that resulted in an international crisis and brought the world to war also brought its repercussions to Swindon. The Great Western Railway, like all other railways in the land, had extra burdens and duties laid upon it by the demands of war. The factory at Swindon had government warwork contracts to fulfill and fewer men to do it. It was a case of all hands to the deck all the time! A general stoppage of work for a week was not only impracticable, it was impossible. *The Railway Magazine* supported this view, stating, 'it is necessary they should go on working at full pressure throughout the summer'. As well as all this the urgent requirements of the military authorities for the transport of supplies, equipment and men by rail, made great demands on the Traffic Department, making it impossible for them to find the necessary coaches and engines for the customary excursion, let alone the men to fire and to drive them. The Council for the Mechanics' Institution issued notices to the effect:

> The Council regret to announce that on account of the war it is not possible to make arrangements for running the 'trip' in July. The matter will, however, be reconsidered later with a view to ascertaining if the event can take place in September or early in October.

1915 was a time when Britain was still optimistic that the war would soon end. Unfortunately, their optimism was ill founded and it would be another four years before TRIP was resumed.

1919

The resumption of TRIP had to await until the ending of hostilities and the return of men and traffic to normal railway duties. Despite the relief and celebrations to mark what was said to be 'the war to end all wars', it was too late to organise the event for 1918 but the welcome news of its reinstatement was heralded afar by the GWR's own journal early in July 1919:

A slightly foggy morning in 1920. Comparing this with the pre-war photographs is illuminating. Here the people are dressed more sombrely and hemlines have begun to rise, whilst caps have, sadly, replaced boaters for the men. The rolling stock is painted in the dark red livery, in use from 1912 until 1923, which could look rather dingy when not in pristine condition. It looks as if it has been another rainy start to TRIP. (Brian Arman)

More than twenty two thousand persons, consisting of employees at the GWR Swindon Works and their wives and families, will leave Swindon by special trains for different parts of the country on July 4th for the annual 'trip'. The holiday will last eight days during which time the Works will be closed.

7,000 chose destinations in the West of England with almost 5,000 going to Weymouth and some 2,000 to the north of England. The holiday period was, surprisingly, for eight days, during which time the works remained closed.

Amongst these celebrating holidaymakers were many young women who worked for Garrards Engineering Co., established in Swindon during the First World War, manufacturing light mechanical engineering products such as gramophone motors. In the period after the war, Garrards made the decision to fix their annual works holiday for the first week in August despite the fact, as was pointed out to them, that TRIP was early in July. However, when the time came and the managing director of Garrards found 'many of his workpeople with Great Western free passes in their pockets were away for Trip week *and* Garrard's own holiday', he made sure in subsequent years that the holiday periods were the same! Once again, the power and influence of TRIP prevailed.

1924

A staggering 29,000 people made up of 19,000 adults and 10,000 children departed Swindon on 3 July and 4 July in thirty-one Special Trains comprising 520 coaches, all entrained in less than eight hours. What a record! *The Railway Magazine* reported it as, 'the biggest excursion in the world'. The GWR's own journal was much more prosaic. It merely reported that, '29,000 of the employees and their families took advantage of the facilities granted by the Directors through the Mechanics Institution and travelled by TRIP Trains to places all over the Company's system'. It seemed to find it more interesting that some also travelled 'by through trains to towns on other companies' lines'. This was the highest record throughout the life of TRIP. Whether it was to do with the hot weather the country was having – the *Swindon Advertiser* reports that 11 July was 'The Hottest Day of the Year' – or whether it was because people were keen to make full use of something that was free when jobs were possibly under threat (the *Swindon Advertiser* also reports that unemployment has returned and that 300 people are registered at the Swindon Employment Exchange), the fact is that the number of Trippers was up by 2,000 on the year before: a significant increase.

1925

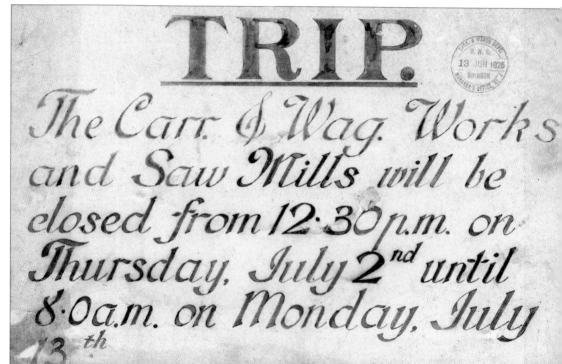

Above: This thin and faded poster of 1925 is of particular significance as it carries the immortal word, 'TRIP'.

Opposite: The world record-breaking numbers, 29,000, that went on TRIP in 1924, created a Herculean task in respect of co-ordinating and managing TRIP Trains without interfering with everyday and extra summer traffic. It was a magnificent feat but created a huge headache for the company, which they described as, 'an extremely difficult working problem.' Obviously this year, 1925, they want to alleviate that problem.

GREAT WESTERN RAILWAY

Annual Leave Arrangements.

Last summer very great difficulty was experienced by the Company in dealing with passenger train traffic, particularly during the week-ends.

With the view of easing the position this year the members of the staff are earnestly requested to be so good as to consider **how far it will be possible for them to commence and terminate their holidays and railway travel during the middle of the week, rather than at the end of the week.**

It is hardly necessary to intimate that this request would not be made except to facilitate the working of the traffic and with this reason before them it is hoped that there will be hearty co-operation on the part of the staff in an endeavour to prevent a repetition of what was an extremely difficult working problem last year.

C. B. COLLETT,

Chief Mechanical Engineer's Dept.,
Swindon.
March 1925.

Chief Mechanical Engineer.

JOHN DREW (PRINTERS) LTD., SWINDON.

1930

This year the TRIP period was altered so that the trains were due to pull out of Swindon on Monday 14 July. This new TRIP arrangement was not popular with either holidaymakers or landladies. It was giving the holidaymakers a serious problem, as the seaside landladies were insisting on their usual letting arrangements of Saturday to Saturday. How was the problem to be overcome? Hundreds of the employees, almost 30 per cent of the Trippers according to the *Swindon Advertiser*, resolved not to wait for the Special free TRIP Trains but to use their ordinary 'Priv' (privilege) tickets, and take off on the Saturday. The WBO was inundated with requests and in the end four Special Trains had to be run to cope with the demand. These departed for London, the West of England, the South Coast and Weymouth. The remainder went off on the Monday as had been planned.

Page 2 of this booklet informs us that 14,381 adults and 6,850 children went away on TRIP this year. It also states that, '*The Annual Free Pass issued to the 47-hour employees in the Swindon factory will not be available on July 2nd, nor during the Works Holiday period except by the Services and Special trains provided*'. The employees had to pay for that part of their journey over other companies' railways.

1932

The *Great Western Railway Magazine* devoted two whole pages to comment on this year's TRIP. It described what it now called 'Swindon Works Annual Holiday' as 'an outstanding event in the life of [this] railway town'. In romantic tones it described the exodus of GWR employees and their families:

> ... the total of 26,000 are transported in a few hours from work to play, from the ceaseless whirl of machinery and the noise and bustle that makes modern life so strenuous to tiny Cornish fishing villages, to the glories of the Lake District, the charm of the Channel Isles, the mountains of Scotland or the gaieties of popular seaside resorts.

It notes that Swindon is very dependent on the Great Western Railway. The Works covers 323 acres and 11,000 persons are employed there. It raises the question, 'what happens to the town when 45 percent of its population is away?' The answer is that if you take a walk down Regent Street, the main shopping thoroughfare of the town, on an average Friday or Saturday evening, it is 'almost impossible to walk in comfort', but on a TRIP day, when the railway families have departed, it is 'practically deserted, scarcely a few dozen people being encountered in its whole length'. The writer makes a very bold statement, declaring, 'It is *probably* the largest excursion of its kind *in the world*'. It is surprising the *Great Western Railway Magazine* did not report this back in 1924!

1933

Great Western Railway Magazine

The exodus comprised 27,416 persons and occupied thirty-one Special Trains; in three and a quarter hours, 23,248 passengers left in twenty-four of the trains. There were 1,031 more trippers than last year. 350 holiday resorts attracted the excursionists. These are the principal ones:

	Adults	Children
Weymouth	3,289	2,203
London	3,142	862
Weston-super-Mare	2,627	1,504
Barry	1,173	860
Teignmouth	562	294
St Ives	533	252
Portsmouth	487	131
Penzance	463	145
Paignton	396	194
Blackpool	459	85
Newquay	426	107
Burnham (Som)	288	181
Jersey	383	85
Tenby	311	121

1938

This was a significant year in the history of TRIP. The Holidays with Pay Act 1938 ensured that every worker was entitled to paid holiday. What a difference this would have made for the Trippers! No longer an unpaid lock-out but a paid break from work. The holiday pay was only for one week and was paid at the flat rate, i.e. without the 'balance' for extra 'piecework'. This meant the railway workers would receive about 50 per cent of a normal pay packet.

1940

With the horror of war came also the shock of once again losing TRIP. Trevor Cockbill recalled it vividly:

> The thought did not occur to me or to any of my friends that the chain of events set in motion by Adolf Hitler posed a threat to the most keenly anticipated yearly event in our lives...
>
> During the night when that false armistice was to take effect, the sirens sounded for the first of Swindon's many night-time alarms. In 19 Dixon Street, we went downstairs and sat huddled in our dressing gowns... By way of diversion, and perhaps because he had been wondering when to tell us, Dad said 'You realise, of course, there'll be no Trip this year!' At first I stared at

him in disbelief, but his expression told us that he was not joking. 'No Trip? No Trip, we *always* go on Trip, every year. Nobody else is not going on Trip…', but Dad interrupted. 'Where did you get that idea from?… As a matter of fact Trip has been cancelled this year, that's official. No Trip trains at all, holidays in the Works are staggered, that means if I get a few days off, it'll be when the gaffer says I can go.' It seemed an inconvenient and unsatisfactory arrangement to me.

Trevor's dad was right. There was to be no TRIP. A 'Special Notice' went up in June in the factory:

Owing to the present Emergency, The Swindon Works Annual Holiday is postponed and any arrangements which have already been made should be cancelled.

It was all very confusing. People were reluctant to believe it. Yet another notice was posted to confirm this (see page 87).

1946
After a lapse of six years, TRIP was reintroduced on 6 July but with a significant difference. It was now not one, but two weeks holiday and with pay! R.J. Blackmore called it 'The Festival of Trip' in his article for the *Great Western Railway Magazine* and so it must have seemed for by this time in its history, TRIP had taken on mythical proportions. It was not just 'making whoppee' or a 'flamboyant outing', to use Blackmore's words. There was, as he so eloquently put it, 'an inexpressible something about it which is finer than that. Somehow there is caught up in it a spirit of nobility – a spirit of solid and dependable family ties.'

The Evening Advertiser announced, 'The First Break Since '39 – With Pay Too'. Zero hour was 2 p.m. on the Saturday afternoon. This was a break with old tradition. Previously, TRIP Trains had had to run in the weekdays so as not to interfere with the weekend holiday traffic. The thinking behind this would have been to tie up with the usual practice for seaside bookings of Saturday to Saturday, as having two weeks out-of-sync would have caused chaos all round.

Although coupon restrictions were still in effect, and such restrictions would have affected our Trippers, the old tradition of something 'new' for TRIP had to be upheld and there was much evidence of new frocks, new shoes and new flannel bags. The Trippers would have had to take their specially acquired emergency rations books with them to give to their landladies, but none of this could dampen the excitement of TRIP's return. As many as 18,000 departed to 'a score or more destinations by as many as thirty Special Trains'. TRIP was truly back, but sadly this was one of the last times that it was run as it had always been, via the Mechanics Institute.

1948
TRIP's 100th birthday! Many changes had occurred over that 100 years and now there was, perhaps, the biggest change of all. It had already been agreed after Labour's victory in the 1945 General Election, under pressure from the freshly emboldened Works Committee, who had long wanted to wrest the privilege of granting passes away from the Mechanics, that the GWR would take over the administration of TRIP from the Institute. Nationalisation made this inevitable. 1948 saw the first TRIP in the nationalised railway era. No longer part of the Great Western Railway Co., Swindon Works was now under the new British Transport Commission. Later it became British Railways, then the Works found itself part of British Railways, Western Region.

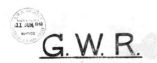

G.W.R.

SPECIAL NOTICE.

THE SWINDON WORKS
HOLIDAY IS POSTPONED INDEFINITELY. THE
ANNOUNCEMENT IN A MORNING PAPER
THAT IT HAS BEEN FIXED FOR
JULY 4TH - 15TH IS INCORRECT.

C.B. COLLETT.

CHIEF MECHANICAL ENGINEER'S OFFICE,
SWINDON.
11TH JUNE, 1940.

No. 44.

GREAT WESTERN RAILWAY
(PRIVATE AND NOT FOR PUBLICATION)

NOTICE
OF

Special Arrangements
IN CONNECTION WITH

SWINDON WORKS
Annual Holiday
1946

All empty and loaded Special Passenger Trains shewn in this Notice must carry " A " Head Lamps ; those running long distances to be formed with corridor stock.

The Trains must be properly marshalled, LAVATORIES FULLY EQUIPPED, AND EACH PORTION LABELLED ACCORDING TO DESTINATION BEFORE EMPTY COACHES LEAVE THE RESPECTIVE DEPOTS WITH LABELS WHICH THE CHIEF MECHANICAL ENGINEER WILL SUPPLY TO THE DEPOT AFFECTED. ON THE FORWARD JOURNEY COACHES AND ENGINES MUST BEAR THE TRAIN NUMBER AS SHEWN IN THIS PROGRAMME. TRAINS FORMED AT SWINDON WILL BE LABELLED BY THE C.M.E. DEPARTMENT.

Swindon Station Master to wire Locodiv, Newton Abbot, and Station Master, Newton Abbot, load in tons of each down special in that direction shewing each portion separately.

SWINDON WORKS HOLIDAYS.

Swindon Works will be closed at 12.0 noon on Saturday, July 6th, and will be re-opened at 7.55 a.m. on Monday, July 22nd.

GENERAL INSTRUCTIONS.

For General Standard Instructions to be observed in connection with the running of the Special Trains shewn in this Notice, see Appendix to Book of Rules and Regulations.

FOR LOCAL ARRANGEMENTS IN SWINDON AREA, SEE SEPARATE RONEO NOTICES ISSUED BY THE DIVISIONAL SUPERINTENDENTS AT BRISTOL AND GLOUCESTER.

Receipt of this Notice to be acknowledged to Head of Department.

GILBERT MATTHEWS,
Superintendent of the Line.

PADDINGTON, June, 1946.
T.20/M.

4459.

Above left: What groans of despair and curses against Hitler and the war this notice would have produced in the Workshops. Mr Collett has learned the lessons from the last war when everyone thought it would be 'over by Christmas' and has sensibly opted for caution – 'postponed indefinitely' says it all.

Above right: TRIP resumes after the interruption of the Second World War – an absence of six years. 17,892 go away on their first holiday with pay.

Right: This poster is interesting because it shows the degree of co-operation with other companies, in this case the Southern Railway, for TRIP. Swindon Town Station had originally been part of Swindon's 'other railway', the Midland & South Western Junction Railway, which was 'absorbed' by the GWR in 1923.

GREAT WESTERN RAILWAY

SWINDON WORKS ANNUAL HOLIDAY 1946
PASSENGERS FOR

SOUTHAMPTON, BOURNEMOUTH, PORTSMOUTH & ISLE OF WIGHT

The SOUTHERN RAILWAY have notified the undermentioned Altered Timing of the 4-40 p.m. SPECIAL ex Swindon Town on Saturday, July 6th which will now run as under :—

		P.M.
Swindon Town	dep.	4.40
Chiseldon	,,	4.50
Andover Jcn.	arr.	5.55
,,	dep.	6.5
Eastleigh	arr.	6.52
Fareham	,,	7.21
Cosham	,,	7.31
Portsmouth & S.	,,	7.49
Portsmouth Harbour	,,	7.54

connecting with 8.5 p.m. Boat from Portsmouth Harbour to Ryde-Isle of Wight.

Southampton and Bournemouth Passengers change at Eastleigh and proceed by Special Train as under :

		P.M.
Eastleigh	dep.	7.0
Southampton Cent.	arr.	7.13
Brockenhurst	,,	7.35
Christchurch	,,	7.54
Pokesdown	,,	8.1
Boscombe	,,	8.5
Bournemouth Cent.	,,	8.10
,, West	,,	8.22

F. W. HAWKSWORTH

Chief Mechanical Engineer's Department,
SWINDON   JULY 1946

GREAT WESTERN RAILWAY
SWINDON WORKS ANNUAL HOLIDAY, 1947.

Midlands & Northern Trains

SPECIAL TRAINS WILL RUN AS SHEWN BELOW:—

Starting from the Station Up Line Platform.

Saturday, July 5th

			Train No. 1	7
			Platform 5	Platform 5
			P.M.	P.M.
SWINDON	...	dep.	1.55	3.32
Banbury	...	arr.	3.18	5.00
Birmingham	...	,,	4.15	—
Wolverhampton	...	,,	4.40	—
Wolverhampton	...	dep.	4.43	—
Wellington	...	arr.	5.15	—
Shrewsbury	...	,	5.35	—
Gobowen	...	,,	6.05	—
Ruabon	...	,,	6.17	—
Wrexham	...	,,	6.27	—
Chester	...	,,	6.48	8.35
Chester	...	dep.		8.40
Warrington	...	arr.		
BLACKPOOL (South)	...	,,		10.22
BLACKPOOL (Central)	...	,,		10.25

On Saturday, July 5th, passengers for OXFORD and the WORCESTER LINE travel by 4.20 p.m. ordinary train from Swindon, changing at Didcot; those for LEAMINGTON and STRATFORD-ON-AVON travel by Special Train No. 1, change at Banbury and proceed by ordinary train.

Passengers for CREWE travel by Train No. 1, change at Wellington proceeding by 5.55 p.m. ordinary train from Wellington due Crewe 7.26 p.m.

Passengers for ABERYSTWYTH travel by Train No. 1, change Shrewsbury proceeding by 6.30 p.m. ordinary train ex Shrewsbury due Aberystwyth 9.50 p.m.

Passengers for OSWESTRY change Gobowen; those for BARMOUTH change at Ruabon proceeding by 7.0 p.m. due Barmouth 9.35 p.m.

Passengers for MANCHESTER travel by Train No. 1, change at Chester, proceeding by 7.8 p.m. ordinary train from Chester due Manchester (Exchange) 8.17 p.m.

Passengers for BIRKENHEAD travel by Train No. 1 in the front part of train, change at Chester, proceeding by 7.0 p.m. ordinary train from Chester due Birkenhead 7.40 p.m.

All passengers for CHESTER must travel by Train No. 1 in the front part of the train and those for BLACKPOOL by Train No. 7.

Passengers for PWLLHELI ONLY may travel by ordinary services throughout.

On any day Sunday, July 6th to Friday, July 18th inclusive, passengers may make the forward journey by any ordinary train.
(NOTE—No Sunday service is available to Aberystwyth or Barmouth).

PRIVILEGE TICKETS DURING HOLIDAY PERIOD.

If Orders are required during the Holiday Period, application, giving full particulars, should be sent to the Manager's Office (Loco. 'r Carriage & Wagon, as the case may be), marked "Privilege Tickets," accompanied by a stamped addressed envelope. In the case of children, the age and sex must be given.

RETURN ARRANGEMENTS.

Passengers must return as shewn below; those from intermediate or branch line stations must connect with the train shewn at the nearest point.

			Saturday, July 12th	Saturday, July 19th
			Train No. 42	53
			P.M.	P.M.
BLACKPOOL (Central)	...	dep.	4.10(A)	4.10(A)
Warrington	...	,,	5.25(A)	5.25(A)
Crewe	...	,,	6.8 (A)	6.8 (A)
BIRKENHEAD	...	,,	4.20(B)	4.20(C)
Chester	...	,,	5.0 (B)	5.0 (C)
Wrexham	...	,,	5.23(B)	5.23(C)
Ruabon	...	,,	5.36(B)	5.36(C)
Gobowen	...	,,	5.51(B)	5.51(C)
Shrewsbury	...	,,	6.28(B)	6.28(C)
Wellington	...	,,	7.00	7.00
Wolverhampton	...	arr.	7.33	7.33
Wolverhampton	...	dep.	7.43	7.43
Birmingham	...	,,	8.07	8.07
Leamington	...	,,	8.42	8.42
Banbury	...	,,	9.20	9.20
SWINDON	...	arr.	10.50	10.50
SWINDON	...	dep.	11.00	11.00
Wootton Bassett	...	arr.	11.10	11.10

(A) Through coaches Blackpool (Cent.) to Swindon via Crewe and Wellington (Works Holiday free tickets Swindon to Warrington are specially authorised for return over this route by these trains).

(B) Ordinary train between Birkenhead and Wellington, passengers to change to special train at Wellington.

(C) Ordinary train—Through coaches for Swindon will be attached to front of train at Chester and will be transferred to special train ex Blackpool at Wolverhampton.

On Saturdays, July 12th and 19th, ordinary trains in connection with the above services leave Manchester (London Rd.) 4.30 p.m. via Crewe, Barmouth at 2.35 p.m. and Aberystwyth 2.30 p.m.

NOTE: All passengers returning from BLACKPOOL on the Saturdays July 12th or 19th must obtain "Supplementary Tickets" which will be issued without charge at the Regulation Offices, Blackpool Central Station during the holiday weeks.

Passengers from OXFORD and the WORCESTER LINE stations return by ordinary trains through to Swindon.

On any day Sunday to Friday, July 6th to 11th inclusive
" " " July 13th to 18th inclusive
or on Sunday, July 20th
} Passengers may return by any ordinary train.

Passengers travelling by any Trains other than those specified hereon will be required to pay the full Ordinary Fare.

Chief Mechanical Engineer's Dept.,
Swindon.   FIVE.

July, 1947.   F. W. HAWKSWORTH

BOROUGH PRESS, SWINDON.

An interesting document, not least because it is the last time that the Great Western Railway's name will appear in connection with TRIP. Birmingham, Birkenhead and Blackpool were popular destinations for TRIP over many decades.

88

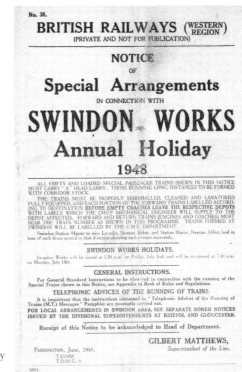

What a landmark TRIP this is. No longer within the Great Western Railway Co., but now part of a nationalised industry, Swindon Works is under British Railways, Western Region. Still TRIP goes on, but sadly no longer administered by the Mechanics' Institution.

1961

The impact of TRIP on Swindon still worked in many wonderful ways, as can be seen from an article in the *Swindon Advertiser* of this date. It reminds Trippers that the '"No fines" privilege ends on Thursday'. It would appear that TRIP holidaymakers received 'privileged' service in respect of their book borrowing in that their fine-free time was extended beyond the usual borrowing period. This was not a one-off concession, as Mr Harold Jolliffe, the borough librarian, explained, but one that had been in operation for the previous fifteen years for the 10 to 15,000 people, to quote Mr Jolliffe, 'a large chunk of the town' that left on TRIP.

1976

It is probable that the last TRIP Special Train ran in this year. The numbers employed at Swindon Works had by this time been greatly reduced to around 3,000. Many of these would now choose to travel to their holiday destination by car or even plane. Those Trippers who travelled by rail would now mainly travel by the regular trains. A British Rail's spokesman's comment to *The Evening Advertiser* in 1979 states, 'Three years ago [1976] we arranged one of two Specials because there were enough employees going to the same place to justify it.' That this was probably the last Special TRIP Train is further borne out by an article in *The Evening Advertiser* of 2 July 1982 when it confirms that, 'It is about six years since British Rail laid on a Special Train because numbers justified it.'

1986

On 26 March 1986 at the end of the afternoon shift, the factory hooter was blown for the last time and the 1,000 or so men who were still employed in the Works walked out for the last time. With no Swindon Works and no railway employees, there would definitely be no more TRIP.

━ CHAPTER FIVE ━

TRIP ORGANISATION ━ 1953

The organising of TRIP was a task of gargantuan proportions. Even in 1953, when the formula had been tried and tested many times, and office equipment and technology was such that administrative procedures were much simpler, it was still a mammoth exercise that took months of preparation. TRIP involved not just the thousands of trippers and their luggage, but also numerous engines, their stabling, cleaning, watering and labelling, coaching stock of different types, timetables made up of an incredible number of departures and arrivals of TRIP Trains and local Specials, all of which had to be fitted around the schedules of everyday Passenger and Freight trains.

By 1953 British Railways had been in existence for a handful of years. Swindon Works was part of British Rail, Western Region. Those in high places labelled the event WAH ━ Works Annual Holiday, but to those who worked 'Inside' and their families, it was still TRIP ━ as it was to the rest of Swindon. It was, however, no longer the prerogative of the Mechanics' Institution to handle all the arrangements, but now rested on the shoulders of the staff section in the Works General Offices.

ADMINISTRATION

By 1953 the Chief Mechanical and Electrical Engineer's job had for sometime been delineated and now three men did the job of the previous one, of whom R.A. Smeddle was the mechanical and electrical engineer, Swindon, whilst C.T. Roberts enjoyed the title and role of carriage and wagon engineer, Swindon. It was to these two men that K.W.C. Grand, Chief Regional Officer (Western Region) of the Railway Executive, Paddington, sent a memo dated Friday 20 February 1953, stating:

Swindon Works Annual Holiday ━ 1953
It has been agreed to close the Works at Swindon for the two week summer holiday from 5.20 p.m. on Friday 3rd July until 7.40 a.m. Monday 20th July, and I shall be glad to receive authority to proceed with the necessary arrangements, in conjunction with the Operating Superintendent, in connection with the running of the annual excursion trains for the workmen and their families.

Here we can see the Staff Office building. Built in 1869 by Joseph Armstrong with the top storey added by Churchward in 1904, the ground floor was where No.13 Staff Office with the Travel Section was housed. In the foreground is the Bristol down line on the left and on the right the London up line. The sidings from which Trippers would depart can be seen alongside the buildings on the left of the picture, which run beside B Shed and the Works' Telephone Exchange.

It was the first step in the administrative process. From now until after the final review there would be memos, notices, letters, instructions, counter-instructions, information booklets and posters flying around the Works as well as to and from Paddington and other places up and down the line of Western Region.

Each year the reality of TRIP was established through an administrative procedure. It was given a file number. This reference number was to be used on all correspondence relating to TRIP. Once this number was created, TRIP had an identity. In 1953 this number was 3962 13/1. 3962 was its own individual file number whilst 13 was the Staff Office. The /1 identified all Staff activities within 13 Office, not just travel. Bertram (Bert) Carter was the clerk-in-charge of Staff Office, and it was his signature or initials that appeared at the bottom of most pieces of administration communications, signing on behalf of R.A. Smeddle and C.T. Roberts. William (Bill) Harris was the clerk-in-charge of Travel Section and it was this section that dealt with TRIP.

A great number of people were involved and had to be kept informed in respect of the happenings and progress of TRIP requirements and arrangements. Names that were significant on the 1953 correspondence besides Smeddle, Roberts and Grand were W.N. Pellow, Motive Power Superintendent (the third in the re-constructed CMEE's job) H.G. Johnson, Manager of the C&W Works, J.J. Finlayson, Manager of the Locomotive Works, H.W. Gardner, Assistant to Chief Accountant, all at Swindon, and Gilbert Matthews, the Operating Superintendent, Paddington. However, as planning and preparations took shape and the details grew longer and more complex, and as the time until departure date grew shorter, the number of people who 'needed to know' grew longer. Minutes of a meeting held in connection with TRIP arrangements on Friday 19 June identify those present as:

Mr. H.E. Hallett, Asst. Dist. Operating Supt Bristol (Chairman),

Mr. H. Morris and Insp. Fowler O.S.O. Paddington,

Mr. I. Coggins, Mr. H. Hobbs, Insp. Hodge, Insp. Bray D.O.S.O. Bristol.

Mr. D. Reynolds Asst. D.M.P.S. Bristol

Mr. H. Maggs, D.M.P.S.O. Bristol,

Mr. R .S. Wiltshire, M.P.S.O. Swindon,

Mr. S. Morgan, Mr. W. Allen, Mr. G. Boffin - Motive Power, Swindon,

Mr. H. Colton, Mr. S. Herbert, Mr. A.

Turner, Mr. W.H. Trueman, - C.&W. Dept, Swindon,

Mr. E. Row, Mr. S. Matthews - Loco Works, Swindon,

Mr. W. Harris, M. & E.E and C. & W. Dept., Swindon (Staff Office, Travel Section),

Mr. H. R. Webb, Swindon Town,

Mr. H. Sharples, Station Master, Swindon Junction,

District Insp. Cotterill, Swindon,

Mr. W. Pratt, Goods Agent, Swindon.

Others who regularly received instructions from Gilbert Matthews, O.S.O. Paddington, were those in charge of significant stations up and down the line including:

L. Edwards, District Operating Superintendent, Bristol,

N.H. Briant, Paddington,

W.R. Stevens, Newport,

D.M. Turnbull, Cardiff,

J.F.M. Taylor, Swansea,

D.L. Pride, Birmingham,

A.J. Robinson, Exeter,

C.F.E. Harvey, Plymouth,

R.H.B. Nicholls, Gloucester,

F.G. Dean, Worcester,

L. Hamblin, Chester,

T.C. Sellars, Oswestry.

In preparation for the mammoth task ahead and in anticipation of the mountain of paperwork that it would generate, a memo was dispatched on 27 February from the C&W engineer's office to H.W. Gardner, requesting him to supply:

12,000 Foolscap envelopes,

2 boxes rubber bands (large size)

2 boxes rubber stamps (small size)

2 boxes wire clips.

It was still a time of austerity and Swindon Works were still using the practice, started in the war period, of using both sides of the paper – that is not just turning over to carry on, but re-using paper that had previously been used on only one side. They would also cut the paper in half if it was just a short note or memo, so a lot of the correspondence relating to the year 1953 appears on the back of correspondence relating to something else.

But we are a little ahead of ourselves in the chronology of events. Internally the first staff to receive instructions as to requirements for travelling on TRIP were:

T.H. Turner, Esq.,

Mr E.C.G. Wood,

F.C. Mattingley, Esq.,

Mr T. St J. Besant,

S.C. Bown Esq.,

Mr M. Jones,

W.N. Pello, Esq.,

Mr. J.L. Booker,

H.G. Johnson, Esq.,

Mr Jenkins,

Mr H.G. Coleman,
J.W. Innes, Esq.,
Mr S.R. Yates,
J.J. Finlayson Esq.,
Mr R.J. Harding,
R.W. Dawe, Esq.,

H.W. Gardner, Esq.,
Mr W. Challenger,
Mr R.C. Lee,
Mr T.L. Whipp,
Mr B.H. Carter,
Miss E. A. Gutteridge.

Here, in splendid isolation, we see Miss E.A. Gutteridge, formally in charge of the Telephone Exchange, but in this instance the Women's Welfare Supervisor. She stands out as the only woman included in TRIP organisation at this level.

Each of these persons received a copy of the same, very specific instructions in respect of receiving 'yellow' application forms for, 'free tickets in favour of Clerical and Supervisory staff so entitled'. It was pointed out that this was an additional free ticket which was granted as 'a special domestic arrangement outside the quota authorised by the Railway Executive'. It was also pointed out that this was a local issue that was, 'confined to the boundaries of the Western Region as at present constituted'. By 1953 TRIP was open to all Works' employees, but this additional Free Pass for use on trains during TRIP was not. This was still a privilege, as previously, for those who had been members of the Mechanics Institution. The Memo was extremely emphatic that these tickets 'are only granted to Clerical or Supervisory staff who were members, of the Mechanics Institute before 7 June 1931 and are still members'. Staff who had transferred from the manual to the clerical or supervisory since then were not (this last word was underlined to make the point more strongly) entitled to the additional pass and should not be given an application form. Even more emphatically, it states:

... no application for free tickets on the pink forms will be accepted unless and until a white application form, for a free ticket which will be stamped 'S' has been submitted.

It warns that, 'this directive [is] to be scrupulously adhered to'. It also warns that the free tickets will only be issued to the boundaries of the former Great Western Railway; for journeys travelling further, the final destination must be shown and an 'interchange privilege ticket order will be issued'. On top of this, those who were desirous of having relatives or friends accompany them had an extra set of forms to fill out for these people. The instructions also stated that those staff wishing to travel by the Works Annual Holiday Special Trains, i.e. TRIP Trains, using their Annual Leave Free Tickets or Privilege Tickets, would require a special permit authorising them to travel. All completed applications for the various tickets and permits had to be returned along with a list giving:

1) Names of persons travelling (including dependants accompanying them)
2) Destination and route where necessary
3) Dates of forward and return journeys.

For those staff wishing to use their Annual Leave ticket or Privilege Tickets, their requests had to reach No.13 Staff Office by Thursday 16 April. It was a very robust document.

The first administration difficulty to be dealt with was that of getting authorisation for waiving the restrictions placed on the use of Free and Privilege Tickets to the Channel Islands during the months of July, August and September. The Channel Island services were now under the authority of the Southern Region and representations needed to be made to them to waive these restrictions for Trippers returning via Weymouth on either of the two Saturdays within

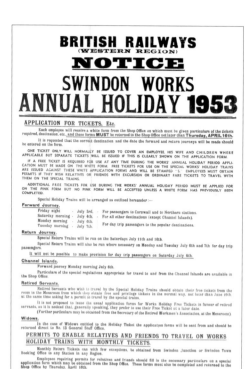

What excitement would have run through the Works and stations when this poster went up. This would be the first visible communication that TRIP preparations were in hand. Instructions and information are given in very concise detail.

the holiday period. This point was duly raised and the need for immediate action noted in a memo of 20 February. A memo on Friday 8 April confirms agreement to this request. It goes on to point out, however, that the Swindon staff will not get priority treatment, and that, 'they will be dealt with on the same basis as the public in this respect'.

COMMUNICATIONS – NOTICES

In order to get the relevant information to the would-be Trippers, and in order to extract the required information from them, it was necessary to have a communication system. A tried and tested system that been operational over the decades of TRIP was 'the Notice'. Whatever form it took, it was an essential cog in this well-oiled machine. Notices, whether as posters, leaflets or booklets, were all part of the armoury to advise, inform and instruct Swindon Trippers of the necessary details in relations to the different aspects of going on TRIP. Information and instructional notices would need to be sent out to all the workshops and stations throughout the preparations. Early on, the notice posters would be to let people know of the general arrangements being made so that they could comply with the requirements in good time. A note sent to the Station Masters at Highworth, Stratton, Wootton Bassett, Purton and Chiseldon, dated 17 March, states:

I enclose a poster setting out the general arrangements being made in connection with the Swindon works Annual Holiday in July next, and shall be very much obliged if you will arrange for it to be exhibited at the station for the information of the retired members of the staff residing in the District.

The total number of notices and posters needed was large. On 18 June the Borough Press invoiced for the following order:

200	Trip Annual Posters	£5 10s 0d
200	Interchange Tickets Posters	£4 3s 6d
200	Local Services Posters	£7 15s 0d
8,100	Annual Holiday Train Notices	£35 15s 0d
Total		£53 3s 6d

Information and procedure notices would bear the names of R.A. Smeddle and C.T. Roberts at the bottom. Notices of train arrangements of particular Districts carried the name of that District Operating Superintendent. Notice No.G247, for Gloucester District, carried R.H.B. Nicholls. The notice of Special Arrangements for TRIP bore the name of the Operating Superintendent. In 1953, Special Arrangements Booklet No.35 bore the name of Gilbert Matthews.

A5 in size and thirty-two pages in content, it covered everything to do with the trains connected with TRIP. Here, the mass of specific details relevant to each and every journey was communicated in a concise and understandable form. It was a major work in its own right. A 1953 copy bears the red ink signature of W. Harris of No.13 Staff Office. It is still a work in progress and Mr Harris' red ink comments and crossings out can be seen throughout the booklet along with other people's pencilled corrections and ink-written comments.

The booklet contained all manner of information and instructions. There were instructions as to how the trains were to be got ready:

Properly Marshalled, Cleaned And Lavatories Fully Equipped And Each Proportion Of The Forward Train Labelled According To Destination

There were exact details of the make-up of each individual train, e.g. for the trains travelling from Swindon to Cornwall:

Train No.1 conveys passengers to St. Ives only.
Formation: Brake third, 7 Thirds and Brake Third (270 tons).
Train No. 2 Conveys passengers for Liskeard, Looe, Par,
St.Columb Road, Newquay and Perranporth,
Formation: Brake Third, 8 Thirds, Brake Third, (300 tons).

It detailed the timetables and numbers of passengers for outward journeys:

Saturday 4th July SWINDON TO PADDINGTON (No. 7 SPECIAL)
depart Swindon Junction 6.27am – Steventon 6.52 – Didcot 6.56 – arrive
Reading 7.17, depart 7.25, Slough 7.45, Southall 7.55 arrive Paddington
8.10 am; 21 adults and 5 children for Reading and 950 adults and 206 children for Paddington

There were also the details for return journeys:

Saturday 11th July PADDINGTON TO SWINDON (No. 39 SPECIAL) 854 adults and 161 children depart Paddington 7.55pm, Southall 8.8, Slough 8.17, arrive Reading General 8.37, depart 8.45, Didcot 9.6, Steventon 9.11, arrive Swindon Junction 9.36pm.

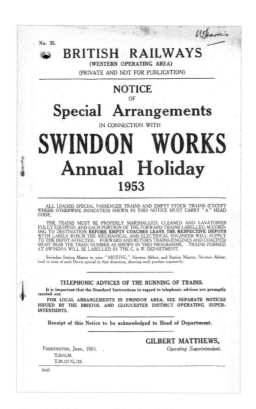

Above left: This copy of the Special Arrangements Booklet, obviously still in draft stage, is that of W. Harris (see name written in top right hand corner) in No.13 Staff Office, and has his red-ink comments and crossings out throughout it, along with other people's pencilled corrections and ink-written comments.

Above right: Still in the process of amendment, here there are three different sets of corrections and comments. Those in pencil relate to the numbers that can be accommodated in the different coaches. The black ink writing says – '*Cannot get more than 10 or in certain cases 11 coaches into Portsmouth Harbour Station*'. Mr Harris comments in red, state, '*Not sufficient accommodation and made worse by providing first class coaches Spoke to Operating Supts. Office several times on this*'.

The booklet also had notes giving fuller explanations of the make-up of the passengers, what would be happening at the various stops, and what the empty stock should do. In regard to those 950 adults and 206 children passengers travelling on the Special to Paddington, it informed:

> Includes about 56 passengers for various destinations in South-East England, who travel by Special Train No. 7 to Paddington and thence by ordinary services from Southern Region London Stations. Also about 586 passengers for Eastern Region via London. Empty stock to Old Oak Common.

Finally, it also detailed the timetables, routes and requirements for disposal of the empty stock of forward Special Trains and the same for the return Special Trains. It was a triumph of meticulousness, and the final, complete booklet was something that any Operating Superintendent would be proud to put his name to.

TICKETS

Another of the elements that made up the complexity of the organisation of TRIP was that of the issuing of tickets. TRIP required many thousands of these and thousands of different application forms to apply for them. An invoice from Messrs Twitchers & Co. identifies that over 25,000 application slips for holiday tickets had to be printed as well as 4,500 permits.

All those travelling on TRIP had to be issued with appropriate tickets and permits. This was a job that, even to those whose everyday work was nothing else but dealing with Works employees' Privilege Ticket requirements, must have seemed a daunting task. One, as the *Great Western Railway Magazine* in 1936 put it, 'to be tackled with a stout heart and plenty of patience'. The Works Booking Office, or Priv. Office as it was known, was situated at the tunnel entrance at Emlyn Square. It was only opened at specific times. Schedules for 1953 identify that this would be open each day the week before TRIP, starting from Friday 26 June with opening hours between 12.15 and 1.30 p.m. and again between 4.14 and 6.30 p.m. Messrs Cavalot, Harris, Middleton, Wakeley, Partridge, Couzens and Meek, along with Mrs Little and occasionally Miss Dawes, were assigned to this duty. On Friday 3 July, the day before the big departures, the office also opened between 10 and 11 a.m. in order to ensure everyone had their tickets.

Each application form was coloured white, yellow (or buff) pink, or blue to identify the different types of pass or ticket. Widows of deceased employees, for example, used a blue form.

DAY EXCURSION TICKETS

These were a special arrangement for friends and relatives of employees and could be used on some Special Trains. File correspondence from Gilbert Matthews confirms the agreement of Mr Furber that Day Excursion Tickets were to be issued:

> for the use of friends and relatives of the Works Employees to those destinations to which special trains are being run on Monday and Tuesday July 6th and 7th.

and a note to Mr E. Sharples, Swindon Junction Station Master, confirms that Day Excursion Tickets can be issued for Weston-super-Mare on 6 and 7 July.

OTHER TICKETS

As if all this was not enough, tickets for accompanying baggage, such as dogs, bicycles, perambulators and motorcycles, had also to be applied for. The costs of these were based on the mileage from Swindon by the shortest route, with tickets available for 10, 15, 30, 50, 75, 100, 150, 200 and 300 miles. A blank was left to be filled in for distances over 300. (Details available for 1954 show that taking the pram cost F. Marsh and W. Ogbourne 6s 3d each.) A room in the Mechanics' Institute was used to deal with the applications and tickets for Luggage in Advance, and appropriate insurance was also offered.

PRIVILEGE TICKETS AND INTER-CHANGE TICKETS (TICKETS OVER OTHER REGIONS)

These had to be specially ordered in from the Operations Superintendent at Paddington, primarily LTE tickets to save congestion at Paddington. Any unused tickets had to be returned

The tickets were individual and date specific and not transferable. On the reverse they carried an extensive amount of information about terms and conditions, and what trains were or were not available to use the ticket on.

back to Paddington together with receipts for those sold. Details as outlined on correspondence dated 20 July identify the numbers of sales of these tickets for two of the regions:

L.T.E. Zone		£ s d
Adult tickets	0569 tickets at 4d each	9 9 8
Child tickets	0141 tickets at 2d each	1 3 6
S.R. Exeter–Weymouth		£ s d
Adult tickets	0090 tickets at 1/2d each	5 5 0
Child tickets	0025 tickets at 7d each	14 7
Total	0825 tickets	16 12 9

The special concession Privilege Ticket, known by all as 'Privs.' whereby the workers would pay only a percentage of the standard fare, was introduced in 1880. Circular No. 572, issued by J. Grierson, General Manager from Paddington Station, informed the workers that:

With the view of affording facilities to persons in the employ of the Company for visiting towns or the country, making purchases, seeing their friends, or for recreation, the Directors have conceded the privilege, under certain regulations, of allowing such persons to travel at a single fare for the double journey, according to class of carriage used.

COLLECTING A 'PRIV' TICKET AT THE 'TUNNEL' ENTRANCE. 1940's GWR WORKS SWINDON

The WBO or Works' Booking Office was one of the most visited places within Swindon Works. Here one would collect one's 'Priv' tickets. Ken Gibbs, who did his apprenticeship in Fitting, Turning and Erecting, and then worked 'Inside' has vivid memories of it and has recaptured them in this evocative sketch.

BRITISH RAILWAYS (Western Region)

Swindon Works Annual Holiday—1954.

Application for Permit to travel on Special Holiday Train.

SHOP............................ Ticket No........................ Name..

Number of Permits Required—Adults........................ Children........................

Names of persons for whom ....
Permits are required

Destination of Special Train........................

Date of Forward Journey........................ Date of Return Journey........................

This form should be completed and returned not later than Tuesday, April 20th.

Everyone who wanted to travel on the Special Trains required a permit. One had to state the date and final destination of the forward and the return journeys. This was to ensure that each Special Train make-up was suitable for the number of passengers to that specific destination.

BRITISH RAILWAYS (Western Region)
Swindon Works Annual Holiday—1954.

● Application for Holiday Tickets

Shop or Office .... Name ....

DESTINATION	Forward Date	Return Date	TICKETS REQUIRED FOR:— (Enter number e.g. (ONE) in appropriate column)							No. of Mechanics' Institute Membership Card (See Note D)
			Self	Wife	Dependent Children				House-keeper (see Note C)	
					Under 21 years (see Note A)		21 years and over (see Note B)			
					Male	Female	Male	Female		
If not residing in Swindon give Station travelling from to join Special Train.										

NOTE A.—Under the age of 21 years; permanently resident with applicant and not earning more than 35/- gross per week or the equivalent of that amount.

NOTE B.—21 years of age or over and permanently resident with and wholly dependent upon the applicant. **NOT** applicable to sons or daughters temporarily out of employment.

NOTE C.—Applicant must state relationship of Housekeeper. Ticket can only be issued **if previously granted.**

NOTE D.—Supervisory and Clerical Staff who were transferred to these grades or became members of the Mechanics' Institution since 7th June 1931, **are not entitled to Annual Holiday Tickets.**

Signature ....

This form to be completed and returned not later than Tuesday, April 20th.

Staff applying for the Mechanics' Institute Pass used this form. This was to apply for a third-class Works Annual Holiday free ticket. This was only issued to the boundaries of the former Great Western Railway, although the intended final destination had to be shown in order that an interchange Privilege ticket order could be issued to complete the journey.

BRITISH RAILWAYS (Western Region)
Swindon Works Annual Holiday—1954.

	FOR OFFICE USE
	State whether old or new free ticket conditions

● Application for Ordinary Free Ticket during Holiday Period

SHOP .... Ticket No. .... Name ....

DESTINATION	REGION	Forward (Actual Date of travel)	Return (Actual Date of travel)	TICKETS REQUIRED FOR:— (Enter number e.g. (ONE) in appropriate column)					
				Self	Wife	Dependent Children			
						Under 21 years (see Note A)		21 years and over (see Note B)	
						Male	Female	Male	Female
If not residing in Swindon give Station travelling from to join Special Train.									

NOTE A.—Under the age of 21 years; permanently resident with applicant and not earning more than 35/- gross per week or the equivalent of that amount.

NOTE B.—21 years of age or over and permanently resident with and wholly dependent upon the applicant. **NOT** applicable to sons or daughters temporarily out of employment.

Signature ....

This form MUST be completed and returned to the Shop Office not later than Tuesday, April 20th.

Staff who were *not* entitled to the Works Holiday free ticket would submit this form to apply for an Ordinary Free Ticket to use during the holiday period but they still required a permit for travelling on a Special TRIP train.

These tickets were not a 'right' of the worker, but issued at the discretion of the Co. , 'only under special circumstances'. Circular H289, dated 5 May 1926, during the General Strike, indicates how tightly the company controlled them. It states:

> Privilege tickets may be issued to members of the loyal staff in cases of emergency only, such as serious illness or death in the family, but on no account to those on strike.

In later years the amount paid was reduced to half the single fare for the double journey.

FACILITIES

During TRIP many types of carriages were brought into service and so many Trippers would find themselves travelling on old-fashioned stock without any 'facilities', i.e. refreshments or even toilets on board. Comfort stops (what was known as LPs – Lavatory Purposes) at appropriate stations had, therefore, to be incorporated into travelling plans.

In 1953 the Employee Side of the Works Committee made an inquiry as to whether it would be possible for arrangements to be put in place for light refreshments of tea and coffee to be served from the brake van of the various long-distance trains. A reply from the Hotels & Catering Services on 9 March, however, stated that they would be pleased to make arrangements for the provision of a station trolley service. Towards the end of May, Mr Smeddle writes to E.K. Portman-Dixon, responsible for the Hotels & Catering Dept., hopefully requesting that, 'as in previous years, arrangements can be made for the provision of refreshments to passengers travelling on the Special trains'. Again on 25 June, Mr Smeddle takes up the matter and again puts the request to the H&C's Superintendent's Office, but it would appear it was left a little late in the day. This was pointed out in no uncertain terms, 'I am afraid you have left it too late for me to make such heavy arrangements at such short notice… (but) an urgent attempt will be made.'

However, Mr Smeddle was anxious that the Employees Side of the Works Committee were aware that efforts had been made on their behalf and that their request had not been neglected or overlooked. Missives flew thick and fast between the relevant offices but it was to no avail. The timing was too short to take on board the casual labour that was usually used in these instances for the outward journeys and, although the Hotels Executive had offered to look at the return journeys, the Works Committee wrote to Smeddle on 2 July, saying that, 'whilst the Committee and I are appreciative of all the efforts that been made', it was perhaps wiser to 'drop the whole question for this year' as, because of the lateness of decision, the arrangements may not be 'sufficiently patronised' and 'jeopardise an application being made next year'. It was decided that the matter should be noted and given much earlier attention the next year. Mr Smeddle makes this point strongly in his letter of 14 August to the Refreshments Room Superintendent's Office, stating, 'I will write to you as early as possible in the New Year with regard to providing buffet service from the brake vans of long distance trains in connection with the Works Holiday in 1954'. Obviously, he was not going to let them tell him off again.

EXTRAS

Swindonians, other than Swindon Works' employees and their families, were, with suitable dispensation, allowed to travel on the Special Trains. Early in March a standard letter was sent out to 121 GWR widows inviting them to complete the enclosed application (blue) form for a

Swindon Works Annual Holiday
1953

INTERCHANGE
PRIVILEGE TICKETS

The following additional Interchange Privilege Tickets will be sold from the Works Booking Office.

Stations	Fares		Tickets to be obtained at Window No.
	RETURN FARE		
	Adult	Child	
LONDON TRANSPORT EXECUTIVE Paddington to Euston, St. Pancras, Kings Cross, Liverpool St., Fenchurch St., Marylebone, Victoria, London Bridge, Waterloo.	4d	2d	**3**
SOUTHERN REGION Exeter to Exmouth.	1s 2d	7d	**2**

These Interchange Privilege Tickets will be available for travel on any date between the 3rd and 19th July (incl.) and can be obtained from the Works Booking Office on Wednesday, Thursday and Friday, July 1st, 2nd and 3rd during the following hours:—

	a.m.	p.m.	p.m.
Wednesday, July 1st	10.0 – 11.0	12.30 – 1.30	5.20 – 6.15
Thursday, ,, 2nd	10.0 – 11.0	12.30 – 1.30	4.15 – 6.15
Friday, ,, 3rd			

These tickets will only be issued on production of a Privilege Ticket Order indicating travel between the above named stations.

Mechanical and Electrical and Carriage and Wagon Engineers' Departments, SWINDON.   JUNE, 1953

R. A. SMEDDLE
C. T. ROBERTS

The Swindon Press, Eastcott Hill, Swindon

This notice gives information about additional Interchange Privilege Tickets. Privilege Tickets were a concession granted initially by the Great Western Railway but were also kept on after Nationalisation. They could only be obtained from the Works Booking Office in the tunnel entrance.

BRITISH RAILWAYS — THE RAILWAY EXECUTIVE
WESTERN REGION   3016

Requisition and Return of Specially Printed Excursion, Cheap or Special Trip Tickets   *Please quote this reference*

No. of Passengers.............Guarantee £.............Name.............

TRIP NUMBER E 213

The undermentioned Specially Printed Tickets enclosed are for issue on date shewn. You will be advised by your Superintendent of the Fares to be charged. The Tickets and the Fares (when printed on them) must be examined immediately they are received and compared with this Requisition, and should any discrepancy appear, the Audit Section must be immediately advised thereof.

TO These particulars must be entered in full on the Classification	ROUTE	Back No.	Colour	Date of Trip		Number of Tickets supplied	Number of Tickets returned	Number of Tickets issued	Fare	Receipts	Month accounted for	REMARKS
				Forward	Return	3rd Class	3rd Class	3rd Class				
				EXCURSION SPECIAL TRIP		FARES ... TO BE PRINTED					For Audit use only	
St Davids				Privilege Rtn								
,,	Topsham	10		July 4	July 4	150		z	1 2			
					Child	50		z	7			
TOTALS						200						

Issues and Receipts to be accounted for in Other Reduced Excursion Column of Classification.

Commission @ .... £.......s.......d........ Allowed to.............. Date .... R.F.C. No..............

Advice of Trip .... No.......

The above-mentioned Tickets must be sent to the Station on or before ....

By .... Train

For C. R. DASHWOOD..............

I hereby certify that the quantity of Tickets received, issued and returned, agree with the particulars stated as above, and that the total Receipts were remitted to .... on.............. 19..........

.... Station Master

The unsold Tickets and Vouchers with this Return enclosed must be forwarded to the Audit Section, Paddington, as a Value Parcel properly labelled with Audit Number shewn on Address Label 526A., specially provided for unused Excursion, etc., Tickets. This Return must be sent by the next train leaving the Station after departure of the last Excursion or special Trip Train for which the Tickets have been provided.

S—To be filled in by the Station Master.

This is one of the very few official documents that actually has 'Trip' printed on it so, whilst not visually very exciting, it is of great historical significance.

free ticket for themselves and any children who qualified under the conditions as set out. These tickets allowed them to travel by any of the Special Trains that would run on the Friday night, 3 July, and on Saturday morning, 4 July, or take the day-trip trains on Monday or Tuesday 6 and 7 July or travel on Saturday 11 July. Relatives and friends wishing to accompany the family, upon completion and return of a second application form, would be able to obtain 'monthly return tickets from Swindon Junction or Swindon Town Station Booking Offices, to any station on any region of the British Railways'.

The Revd B.P Barnes of 22 Chester Street wrote, in a type-written letter, on 19 May, to Mr Smeddle requesting such dispensation. He says:

> May I have the necessary permission for myself and twenty-one Scouts of the 4th Swindon, Saint Mark's Scout Troop to travel on the Ilfracombe Trip Train on Saturday, July 4th as far as Mortehoe Station. We are going into North Devon for our Annual summer camp.

He points out that, 'some of the Scouts work for the railway and of the others, most of their fathers are employed by Western Region'. Revd Barnes was obviously aware that this was rather late in the day to be making such a request and he apologised for that fact and any inconvenience it might cause. He went on, however, to push his luck even further by requesting that should the train be leaving early in the morning, 'it would be a relief to... load up the night before'. A prompt reply the very next day from Mr Smeddle notified Revd Barnes that permission was granted, stating:

> The train you will require will start from the Rodbourne Sidings at 7.10am. (subject to confirmation later) and as the entrance at Rodbourne Lane will be open from about 5.30 a.m. this should give you ample time to "load up". I regret I am unable to give permission for you to enter the Works for this purpose on the evening of Friday the 3rd July.

A further letter to Revd Barnes on Friday 26 June illustrates the attention to detail that was necessary for each individual traveller or party.

> Further to my letter of the 20th may, I enclosed timetable No. 7 which gives details of the Works Annual Holiday Train to Mortehoe, and from which it will be observed that it will be necessary for you and your party to change at Barnstaple.
>
> I confirm arrangements have been made for three compartments to be reserved on train No. 9 for your party.

They were, indeed, lucky to have compartments reserved as it was not usual practice. Other 'extra' passengers were from Garrard Engineering & Manufacturing Co., who had an arrangement with Swindon Works for their employees to use TRIP Special Trains. A response dated 8 May, in answer to a request to confirm that this arrangement still held for 1953, stated:

> ... the arrangements... will be on similar lines to those of last year, and we shall be pleased to provide facilities for your employees to travel on the Special Trains.
>
> I will be obliged if you will let me know your requirements as soon as possible and will send you the necessary permits and leaflets of the actual train arrangements as soon as published.

W.G. Lang, Garrard's Welfare Officer, wrote on 12 June and again on 29 June, requesting, 'Margate 3, Weymouth 3, I.O.W. 2. to be sent as soon as possible'. They were dispatched the very next day – soon enough for anyone, I am sure!

Perhaps the most surprising request is that from a Mr Victor Alexander Puffet of 28 Harding Street. Mr Puffet, a prominent trade unionist and aircraft fitter at RAF Lyneham, resided at the Royal Engineers' Comrades' Club where his wife was stewardess for some fourteen years. He writes, in a very neat hand, as late as 23 June:

> Would you please grant me a permit for my wife and I to travel to Eastbourne on the trip train, July 4th. If you would allow this, would you please, also send the time of the train in enclosed stamped addressed envelope. The friend in the ticket office who usually obtains my Permit is now on holiday.
> Many thanks.
> Yours sincerely

Again, extremely promptly, i.e. the very next day, Mr Smeddle sent the permit and timetable requested. It was good that he did, and that Victor Puffet and his wife were granted their permits to go on their holiday, as it was to be Mr Puffet's last. A small article in *The Evening Advertiser* on Monday 13 July informs of his early death at the age of forty-three from a sudden heart attack on a walk before breakfast. A post-mortem revealed that death was due to natural causes.

STOCK

A huge part of the preparation of TRIP is the consideration of how to make the actual train journeys happen. Once a total figure has been arrived at for each final destination, it is time for the Traffic Department to do their bit. They have to consider not only what numbers of trains and coaches would be necessary, but also what route to go by in order to make the journey happen in the easiest and smoothest possible way without impeding normal traffic arrangements for the general public. A good example of this is outlined in a memo dated Wednesday 21 May, which stated:

> ... in regard to Margate and District... in order to avoid a change of stations in London, a Special Train will be arranged on Saturday July 4th to run via Reading, Redhill and Ashford Junction.
> The Operating Superintendent has made arrangements for a train leaving Swindon at 6.50am arriving Margate approximately 11.20am, but owing to the number of passengers on the return journeys on Saturdays 11th and 18th July being too small, it is not possible to arrange for Return Specials.
> It will be necessary, therefore, as in the case of passengers who travel to Eastbourne and Brighton, for the tickets for the following destinations to be routed 'forward via Reading and Ashford Junction, return via London.

On 8 June the District Operating Superintendent, L. Edwards, based at Bristol Temple Meads, called for a tactical meeting with Smeddle, Roberts, Johnson, Finalyson and Pellow, to discuss:

Stabling of empty trains
Inter-depot working
Cleaning and Watering
Working of local Special Trains (Highworth, Wootton Bassett and/or Purton)
Freight Train Alterations
Stop on inward cripples to Works effective from –

Other meetings covered items such as:

P.L.A. and luggage insurance
Platform tickets
Uniform Police
S.O.L. Ticket Inspectors (in hand with Operating Supt.)
Tail lamps (nos. of from Stores)
Corrections to Printed Proofs

The gathering of empty stock and stabling them on the sidings was regular practice for TRIP. A detailed memo of 19 June states that Sidings Nos 2, 3 and 4 on the Up Side at Rodbourne Lane would be cleared of traffic and ready to receive empty coaching stock from 12 p.m. 27 June and that on the Down Side the Sawmill Sidings would be ready by mid-day Friday 3 July. Others would be stabled at Stratton Park and Marston. However, before the coaches could be stabled, they had to be made ready. Details of a Foremen's Meeting of 15 June lay out specific instructions and identified who was responsible for what. It was agreed that they were to repair and send into traffic all available coaches of the corridor type such as Thirds, Composites and Brake Thirds. These would form Special Trains Nos 2, 5, 7, 9, 11, and 13. (The formation of No.7 Special for Paddington was: Brake Third, thirteen Thirds and Brake Third — 450 tons.) Those coaches that were made available but were not completely finished with had to be marked 'Return to Swindon.' Foreman Lack of No.9 Shop was to arrange to clean out all coaches. Foreman Trueman was to arrange for the supply of steps for trains Nos 5, 9, and 13 leaving Sawmill Sidings and to see to the coupling of coaches and gangways. Foreman Miles was to deal with the clearance of rubbish between Park Lane Entrance and No. 2 Sawmill. Foreman Walker and Foreman Lack to clean and water four trains which will be returned to Military Sidings early on Sunday 5 July for service on Monday 6 July. Foreman Truman was responsible for the labelling of train Nos 2, 5, 7, 9, 10, 11, 12 and 13 and obtaining the labels from Mr B.H. Carter.

The labelling of the coaches was a very important part of the preparations. It was necessary for each coach to be labelled so that the Trippers would know which coach they were to travel in and not get in the wrong one. A note from Mr Roberts gives details of the number of labels necessary for each train and how the coaches were to be labelled.

Train No.405	– Penzance	45 labels
	– Plymouth	5 labels
Train No.421	– Paignton	15 labels
Train No.2	– Liskeard, Par and Newquay	30 labels
Train No.8	– Paddington	52 labels
Train No.10		60 labels dispersed as:
Kingsweir Line (front four coaches)		16
Dawlish Warren & Dawlish (next 2 coaches)		8
Teignmouth & Newton Abbott only (next four coaches)		16
Barnstaple & Bideford (rear four coaches)		14
Passengers joining at Wootton Bassett (3 compartments in first coach)		6

Altogether Mr. Roberts issued 402 labels with this instruction.

A later memorandum identified the distribution of 735 labels over the twenty-three trains involved in main outward journeys.

No. 51

SWINDON

Mr. Frank Gleed collected this coach number on his return TRIP journey in 1955. His sister-in-law, who worked at Garrard, had obtained tickets to Llandudno Junction, as they were going to Blaenau Ffestiniog. The TRIP Special was much easier and cheaper than the normal route which usually involved many changes from Swindon. The train was composed of ex-LMS stock. It left Swindon Junction before midnight and arrived at Llundadno Junction about 6 a.m. after an engine change at Chester and serving other resorts along the North Wales coast. For the return journey the family joined the train at Ruabon. Mr Gleed thinks this window sticker, No.51, was a London Midland Region reporting number as it started from North Wales.

JOURNEYS AND DESTINATIONS

The number of Trippers for 1953 was 15,880 – still impressive number. 15,880 peoples' travel whims and fancies had had to be accommodated, this along with their sudden, and often late, changes of mind for alternative destinations and days of departure. So significant was the 'changing of minds' aspect in 1952 and so undesirable the impact, that a special letter was issued on 7 May drawing the attention of J. J. Finlayson, Esq., and H. G. Johnson, Esq., to this matter:

> Referring to my letter of 13th May 1952, you will be aware that there is no objection to employees making application to change the destination ...but shall be glad if you will advise all concerned that alterations in destinations and dates should be accepted and passed forward to this office as soon as possible after an employee makes known his wishes in this direction.
>
> Despite this instruction being issued last year, consequent on a very large number of alterations received just prior to the holiday it was necessary to place a stop on the issue of tickets and permits for use on certain trains, and I shall be obliged for your assistance in implementing the instruction in the first paragraph in order to avoid a repetition of this nature occurring this year

There is a subtle implied criticism here, highlighted by the underlining, that the lateness of the applications may not have been all on the part of the applicants, but, perhaps, more so on the part of those doing the initial processing.

Whilst there was a decrease in numbers travelling of about 1,750 compared with the previous year, the destinations remained much the same as in the previous year according to an internal letter dated Wednesday May 6. These included: Barry Island, Barnstaple, Bardon Mill, Bexhill Bideford, Birchington, Blackpool, Blue Anchor, Bognor, Braunton, Bradford, Brean Road, Bridport, Bridgewater, Brixham, Broadstairs, Brockenhurst, Bude, Camborne, Canterbury, Cardigan, Carmathen, Channel Islands, Chesterfield, Chichester, Christchurch, Churston, Clacton-on-sea,

Clevedon, Colchester, Colne, Dartmouth, Dawlish Warren and Dawlish, Deal, Derby Devonport, Dover, Dunster, Eastleigh, Falmouth, Fareham, Felixstowe, Filey, Fishguard, Folkestone, Goole, Gorleston-on-Sea, Harrogate, Havant, Hayling Island, Helston, Herne Bay, Horrabridge, Hull, Launceston, Leigh-on-Sea, Leamington, Leeds, Leyburn, Leicester, Lewes, Littlehampton, Lyme Regis, Maestag, Mansfield, Margate, Minehead, Minster, Mortehoe, Mundesley-on-Sea, Newcastle, Newhaven, Newton Abbott, New Milton, Nuneaton, Okehampton, Padstow, Par, Perranporh, Pokesdown, Poole, Porthcawl, Ramsgate, Ripon, Redruth, St Austell, St Columb Road, St. Ives, Sandwich, Scarborough, Scunthorpe Seaton, Sheffield, Sidmouth, Skegness, Southend-on-Sea, Swanage, Taunton, Torquay, Truro, Tunbridge Wells, Tynemouth, Wadebridge, Warrington, Westgate and Whitstable, White Coln, Wolverhampton, Yarmouth and York.

By 16 and 17 June there are schedules of passenger numbers, train numbers, departure places and times, necessary connections to be made, as well as breakdowns of adult and children numbers travelling to specific destinations, and, of course, such details for the necessary return journeys, too.

FORWARD JOURNEYS

The forward journeys began in the late hours of Friday night, departing only from Swindon Junction Station. Only five of these 'overnight' trains left, but they had multiple connections to make.

Train	Time	Destination	Note	No. of Passengers
1	19.55 p.m.	St Ives	passengers for St Ives only. One compartment reserved for passengers joining at Wootton Bassett	400
2	10.30 p.m.	Newquay	passengers for Liskeard, Par, St Columb Road and Newquay will connect at Liskeard for Looe and at Newquay for Perranporth	450
3	11.15 p.m.	Blackpool	passengers for Warrington, Preston, and Blackpool will connect at Preston for Morecambe and stations between Preston and Carlisle	500
4	11.52 p.m.	Birkenhead	passengers for Shrewsbury, Gobowen, Ruabon, Chester and Birkenhed will connect at Shrewsbury for Crewe, Manchester and Liverpool. Will connect at Shrewsbury for Aberystwyth, Barmouth and Pwellheli, will connect at Chester for Rhyl, Colwyn Bay, Llandudno and Holyhead	425
405	11.45 p.m.	Penzance	passengers for Bodmin Road, Lostwithiel, St Austell, Truro, Redruth, Caborne, Gwinear Road, Hayle, Marazion, and Penzance. Change at Bodmin Rd for Padstow and Wadebridge	400

SUMMARY OF PASSENGERS TO BE CONVEYED FROM SWINDON.

	Fri./Sat., July 3rd/4th	Sunday, July 5th	Monday, July 6th	Tuesday, July 7th	Wednesday, July 8th	Thursday, July 9th	Friday, July 10th	Saturday, July 11th	Sunday, July 12th	Monday, July 13th	Tuesday, July 14th	Wednesday, July 15th	Thursday, July 16th	Friday, July 17th	Saturday, July 18th	Total.
West of England	3,234	7	67	25	5	8	26	304	1	27	5	1	6	2	10	3,728
Weston-s-Mare and Burnham	542	12	577	255	89	60	33	95	—	66	109	74	14	44	19	1,989
Weymouth	1,180	14	706	332	55	32	1	134	2	41	27	2	2	—	9	2,537
Channel Islands	—	—	221	—	2	—	12	—	—	1	—	—	—	—	—	236
Reading and London	527	22	283	145	89	92	69	127	9	61	89	75	47	20	20	1,675
Southern Region via Guildford and Redhill	548	—	—	—	—	—	—	—	—	—	—	—	—	—	—	548
Southern Region via London ..	618	19	64	15	9	6	6	90	—	7	7	3	2	—	2	848
Eastern Region via London ..	586	7	15	6	—	1	2	30	—	4	3	13	—	—	—	667
L.M.R. via London ..	13	—	1	2	2	—	—	—	—	—	—	—	—	—	—	18
Southern Region via Andover ..	921	2	52	23	8	—	7	91	2	9	1	3	—	—	—	1,119
South and West Wales	453	2	100	51	15	4	13	28	3	8	10	4	13	—	3	707
Midland and Northern ..	946	7	42	13	10	4	12	68	2	10	13	9	6	—	3	1,145
L.M.R. via Cheltenham, Birmingham and Leeds ..	27	—	7	—	1	3	—	2	—	3	—	—	—	—	—	43
E. & N.E. via Banbury, Leicester and York	228	4	29	6	4	2	4	14	3	6	—	—	—	—	—	300
Scotland	178	1	6	1	3	1	—	—	—	—	—	—	—	—	—	190
Ireland	53	—	10	—	1	—	3	—	—	—	—	—	—	—	—	67
Cheltenham, Gloucester, etc. ..	19	4	14	2	4	—	2	1	—	7	7	2	—	1	—	65
Total	10,073	101	2,194	876	297	213	190	984	22	250	271	186	90	67	66	15,000

Above: Examining the breakdown of the summary highlights some interesting facts. There are Trippers departing every day for the whole two weeks. The second highest number, 2,194, departs on the first Monday, 6 July, although this would have included a good number of 'day trippers'. However, one wonders, how does a Monday start tie up with holiday accommodation's Saturday to Saturday bookings?

Right: The Workmen's Trains ran early on working day mornings to transport the workers from outlying districts into Swindon. It was necessary to bring TRIP travellers in from outlying areas in order that they could take the TRIP Special Trains. It can be seen that some compartments were specially reserved on a number of Specials for Wootton Bassett Trippers off to St Ives, Penzance, Weymouth, Torquay and Weymouth, saving them a journey into Swindon. Wootton Bassett travellers to other destinations would have to travel into Swindon on the Workmen's Trains to get their TRIP Special.

SWINDON WORKS ANNUAL HOLIDAY 1953

Local Services in connection with the Works Holiday Specials will run as under:

THE WORKMEN'S TRAINS
Will run throughout the Holidays, (Mondays to Fridays) July 6th to 17th inclusive.

Lostwithiel for Fowey
Truro for Falmouth and Chacewater
Gwinear Road for Helston
Front two coaches not available for
Swindon Works Passengers

Total 2.175

The fourteen trains that departed on the Saturday started early at 6.00 a.m. and finished at 10.45 a.m. They left from Swindon Junction Station, Swindon Town Station and Rodbourne Lane Sidings (entrance Park Lane).

From Swindon Junction Station

6.25 a.m. for Weymouth	600
6.27 a.m. for Paddington	1,050
6.47 a.m. for Weymouth	600
6.50 a.m. for Margate	575
7.00 a.m. for Plymouth	100
7.20 a.m. for Brighton & Eastbourne	550
7.47 a.m. for Tenby	475
7.52 a.m. for Birmingham	40
0.45 a.m. for Weston-super-Mare	550

From Rodbourne Lane Sidings

6.00 a.m. for Paignton	650
7.10 a.m. for Ilfracome, Teignmouth & Paignton	675
7.55 a.m. for Exmouth & Minehead	625

From Swindon Town Station

8.18 a.m. for Portsmouth & Southsea & Isle of Wight	600
9.55 a.m. for Boscombe & Bournemouth	350
Total	**7,440**

The despatch figures were 'global', rounded up to the nearest five or ten as we can see from looking at the more detailed breakdowns that were prepared for every final destination. The overnight train to St Ives carried 302 adults and ninety-six children, making a total of 398. Of the 400 that set off on the train to Penzance twenty-three adults and fifteen children went to Wadebridge, ten adults to Padstow, five adults to Fowey, just two adults to Chacewater, nine adults and one child to Helston, forty adults and eleven children to Falmouth with 171 adults and thirty-nine actually arriving at Penzance.

There were twenty-four Special Trains for forward journeys for TRIP. Nos 1, 2, 3, 4, and 405 ran on Friday night, 3 July. Nos 9 to 16 inclusive ran on Saturday 4 July. On Monday 6 July four trains, Nos 17, 18, 19 and 20, ran, and Nos 21 and 22 ran on Tuesday 7 July. Finally, Special Train No.421 ran on Saturday 11 July.

Whilst the majority of Trippers, 10,073, left on the first two days of the holiday, there were, in fact, forward journeys to take people on their holiday every day of the two-week period.

Apart from the main TRIP Specials, local 'Special' services had to be arranged to convey passengers from the outlying villages to their TRIP Trains and then back to their villages on their return from their holidays. A notice dated 22 June identifies these.

RETURN JOURNEYS

For some, 1,575 to be precise, the excitement of TRIP was short-lived. The return journeys began as early as Monday 6 July. At 10.10 p.m., 400 weary Trippers departed from Weymouth, followed just thirty-seven minutes later by another 400. 10.38 p.m. saw the departure of 600 from Weston-super-Mare, and 175 left Paddington for home at 11.20 p.m. On Tuesday we have yet another trainload of 350 departing from Weymouth at 10.10 p.m. and 300 more from Weston-super-Mare again at 10.38 p.m. Saturday 11 July and Saturday 18 July saw the bulk of the Trippers return.

Saturday 11 July   No. of Passengers

From	Arr.	No.			
Weymouth	(Swindon) 5.01 p.m.	800	Teignmouth	9.57 p.m.	625
Portsmouth	(Town) 5.55 p.m.	300	Paignton	10.04 p.m.	500
Bournemouth	6.56 p.m.	200	Penzance	10.16 p.m.	550
Paddington	9.36 p.m.	1,025	Blackpool	10.50 p.m.	500

Saturday 18 July   No. of Passengers

From	Arr.	No.			
Weymouth	5.01 p.m.	500	Paddington	9.36 p.m.	1,275
Portsmouth	(Town) 5.55 p.m.	375	Teignmouth	9.57 p.m.	550
Bournemouth	6.56 p.m.	175	Paignton	10.04 p.m.	400
Tenby	7.47 p.m.	350	Penzance	10.16 p.m.	600
Newquay	9.00 p.m.	475			

Once again these are rounded-up figures to the nearest five, but the breakdown details of the numbers brings them back once again to individuals, families, and friends travelling together. For example:

Return Journey Saturday 11 July

West of England	Adults	Children	Total		Adults	Children	Total
Taunton	1	–	1	Bude	11	2	13
Watchet	5	3	8	Dawlish Warren	10	14	24
Blue Anchor	13	6	19	Dawlish	17	19	36
Minehead	31	5	36	Teignmouth	90	19	109
Barnstaple	5	3	8	Newton Abbott	2	–	2
Bideford	56	21	77	Torquay	36	6	42
Mortehoe	2	–	2	Paignton	281	95	376
Ilfracombe	15	3	18	Goodrington			
Exeter	39	10	49	Sands	17	7	24
Littleham	2	3	5	Kingswear	26	6	32
Exmouth	130	67	197	Brixham	6	5	11
Sidmouth	2	–	2	Dartmouth	11	2	13
Seaton	2	–	2	Plymouth	15	1	16
				Total	**825**	**297**	**1,122**

Twenty-one Special Trains were required for return journeys, five of these for separate journeys from Weymouth. Special Train Nos 17, 18, and 19 ran on 6 July. Nos 21 and 22 on 7 July. (There is no identified No. 20.) Nos 36 to 42 inclusive ran on 11 July and Nos 43 to 51 inclusive ran on 18 July. On Saturday 4 and Sunday 5 July, passengers from all points returning on these days had to use ordinary services.

CO-OPERATIONS

TRIP was a masterpiece of co-operations, not only in-house between departments and regions, but also with external organisations and businesses in Swindon itself. Local printers, The Borough Press, located at Eastcott Hill, who described themselves as, 'Printers in many processes, Office Equipment and Furniture', and Twitchers & Co. Ltd were used again in 1953. The Bristol Tramways & Carriage Co. Ltd, (Swindon Branch) was a vital part of the travel plans as was the Passenger Transport Department of the Borough of Swindon, in order to get some of the would-be Trippers to the point of their embarkation. Bristol Tramways agreed, as usual, to run extra journeys in respect of Service 183 – Swindon–Stratton (Circular) early on Saturday morning 4 July, and late night Monday 6, Tuesday 7 and Saturday 11 July. The Borough ran late busses on Friday 3 July, from stops all around the town – Broome Manor Lane, Stratton Cross Roads, Coate Water, Goddard Avenue, Moredon, Haydon Wick, Shrivenham Road and Moredon, up to 11.13 p.m. Their early morning service started at 5am with buses running every ten – twelve minutes along some of the heavy demand routes.

DETAILS

WAGES

The way that railwaymen were paid was always a complicated piece of administration, right from its beginnings. With district rates, different piece rates for different jobs, gang rates, day money, overtime rates, time worked and balance weeks, it was enough to challenge the most nimble of mathematical minds. By 1953 it had become more regularised but no less complicated. A memo from the 1954 TRIP file gives a flavour of the intricacies involved as it advises:

> It will be necessary for the piecework total and Day money in respect of each gang for week ending 3rd July to be furnished to the Central Wages Office by 5.20pm on Friday, 2nd July, in order that the Piecework contract can be agreed with the Chargeman's figures before entry in the paybill.
>
> It is also necessary that copies of the Piecework Certificates for week ending 3rd July be available in the Shop Office should a discrepancy arise.
>
> Details of transfer of wages for the pay on Monday 19th July, and details of men on the night shift week ending 24th July, to be sent to the Cash Office at 7.45pm and 9.0pm respectively.

There were five categories identified for pay arrangements:

A Men entitled 2 weeks HWP and taking 2 consecutive weeks holidays.
B Men entitled to 1 week HWP and out 2 consecutive weeks.
C Men not entitled to HWP but out 2 consecutive weeks.
D Men working during the holiday period.
E Men out ill preceding holiday period. (These received no pay.)
(HWP = Holiday With Pay)

Having worked out what the wages were, special arrangements were made for the handing of it out at the pay tables in the various shops, making sure that the night shift were suitably accommodated. On top of this there were salaries to be paid to supervisory and clerical staff, who were also allowed to apply for advance payment of salary for the holiday period.

LAUNDRY

Whilst Swindon Works holidayed, the rest of the Western Region carried on. However, there were knock-on effects for them. One such effect was in respect of laundry. Swindon had a large Laundry Department which had catered f or GWR's laundry requirements and now still washed and ironed the linen for British Rail's hotels, dining cars and sleeping cars and their various uniforms. A note of 10 June to Mr W. Harris of Travel Section reminded him:

> … will you kindly note there will be insufficient staff to deal with any laundry work …when the Works will be closed for the Annual Holiday, the latest date on which linen and garments for laundering can be received in order that they may be dealt with and returned before the Works close, is Monday 29th June.

STAFFING

Mr. Sharples and District Insp. Cotterrill will provide a Foreman, Parcels Porter, Clerk and two Grade 2 Porters for Swindon Town.
Two Ticket Inspectors will be provided for the Park Lane entrance.
Four uniformed Police will be in attendance at Swindon Junction Station at 8.00 p.m. Friday evening and 5 a.m. Saturday July 5.
The Locomotive Works Watchman to be on duty at the Dean Street Crossing during the entraining periods.

ODDS AND ENDS

To: G. Webb, Station Master Swindon Town Station - From: B.H.C. for Mr. Smeddle. Special Train No. 15 for Portsmouth and Isle of Wight on morning Saturday July this will be made up of first class Southern Region stock. …make arrangements with your staff to ensure that *the arm rests in all compartments are raised before the train is brought into the station in order that the maximum number of passengers may be seated*
Issue of Platform tickets will be suspended at Swindon Junction between 9.00pm Friday July 3rd and 8.00am Saturday July 4th.
Twenty Five Tail Lamps have been ordered from Stores for commencement of programme.

COMPLAINTS

Despite all the planning and meticulous attention to detail, in a project as large as this something is bound to go wrong and, without a doubt, someone will end up complaining. The Monday 13 July edition of *The Evening Advertiser* carried an article, 'Return From Trip', with a sub-heading 'One Complaint'. The reporter, meeting a returning TRIP Train on Saturday 11 July, gathered comments from the many, 'healthy and happy looking trippers'. Two who were not so happy were Mr Storey and Mr P. Scott, who had had to travel back from Weymouth in the guard's van as, according to them, the train was so packed. Mr Storey explained that two trains had taken them there but only one had brought them back. This, on the face of it, would appear to be something of an optimistic arrangement, but many of those who went out on the two trains would not actually be returning until the following week on 18 July. However, the very public and implied criticism stung and correspondence was immediately exchanged to set the matter right. The very next day, R.A. Smeddle despatched a letter to L. Edwards, District Operating Superintendent, Temple Meads Station, Bristol:

> In order to meet any possible complaint which may be made in respect of lack of accommodation… I shall be obliged if you will let me know the reason for the train being made up of 8 thirds, 2 brakes, and 2 compos whereas the formation as shown in Mr. Gilbert Matthew's Notice No. 35 was brake third, 11 thirds, and brake third.

Obviously, the maths here regarding one seat per person do not add up, as:
8 compartments x 8 seats = 64 seats x 8 thirds = 512, + 2 compos + 2 brakes = around 630 seats, whereas 11 thirds = 704 + 2 brakes = around 770 seats.

That the management is very upset by such public embarrassment is apparent from the tone and comments of the letter: 'I have not received any official complaint… but the local press has reported…'. Furthermore, having already established from another enquiry into the matter that there was more than adequate seating available for the 624 passengers they are also somewhat piqued by the seemingly unfairness of the complaint:

> … the guard's journal shows there were 550 passengers on the train and that several compartments had only six people travelling in them, so that the complaint made by the two men in question appears to be unreasonable.

Mr Edward's reply of 23 July, after giving a stout, practical explanation as to the reason in that the heavy seasonal demands of a summer service did not allow for a train to be formed up at Weymouth and kept just for the 1.55 p.m. Special TRIP return, but that it was necessary to utilise the stock forming the 8.52 a.m. Bedminster to Weymouth to cover this, then went on to lay the blame for the difficulty fairly and squarely on the shoulders of the two men:

> It is understood that on the date in question empty compartments were available in the front of the train, but the passengers in the brake van refused to move into that section.

What, one wonders, was the reception that these two poor men received back at the Works, and how badly had they blotted their copy books in respect of their future job prospects? However, their complaint did highlight a difficulty either not foreseen or not thought through, in respect of the running stock, as a pencilled-in, handwritten comment, in regard to the forming up of the trains, highlights, 'This observation must be borne in mind at next year's meetings when formation of trains is being discussed'.

Another complaint about carriage accommodation for 1953 did not actually come to light until application for permits for 1954, when a Mrs Boot of Churchward Avenue writes in a conciliatory, but aggrieved, tone:

BRITISH RAILWAYS

(Western Region)

(For the use of Employees only)

GLOUCESTER DISTRICT

NOTICE OF

PASSENGER TRAIN

ARRANGEMENTS

10th July to 16th July, 1953

Each Station Master must satisfy himself that he fully understands the arrangements shewn herein and is in a position to carry them into effect, also ensure that every permanent member of the staff is instructed with regard to, and understands, the arrangements shewn in this Notice, and, if necessary supplied with a copy.

GENERAL INSTRUCTIONS

For General Instructions to be observed in connection with the running of the Special Trains shewn herein, see the Book of Rules and Regulations, dated January, 1950, and the General Appendix thereto, dated July, 1936.

GENERAL NOTES

For explanation of General Notes, see Service Time Tables.

FOR DETAILS OF THROUGHOUT TIMINGS SEE OPERATING
SUPERINTENDENT'S SPECIAL TRAFFIC NOTICE NO. 5.

SPEED RESTRICTIONS

The Permanent and Temporary Speed Restrictions in operation must be strictly adhered to and the arrangements shewn herein are also subject to alterations and such other special instructions as appear in the Temporary Speed Restrictions, Permanent Way Operations, Signal Alterations, etc., Notices, or any Special Notices subsequently issued thereto.

SPECIAL TRAIN—SWINDON TO PURTON.
"B" Head Code.

Forward.			Arr. P.M.	Dep. P.M.	Return.			Arr. P.M.	Dep. P.M.
Swindon	..	..	—	11 3	Purton	..	..	—	11†30
Loco Yard	..	..	11/ 5		Loco Yard	..	..	11/38	
Purton	..	..	11 12	—	Swindon	..	..	11†40	—

Purton signal box to remain open until Empty Stock has cleared. **District Inspector Drew** to arrange.

Mr Garlick was right to expect a train to take him from Swindon to Purton to complete his TRIP journey as can be seen from this schedule. There was indeed a Special Train designated to run at 11.03 p.m.

Whilst not wishing to be rude, several of my friends and myself would like to put forward a suggestion regarding the 'Trip' train to Newquay. We found that we had quite a comfortable journey getting there, but it was a perfect nightmare on the return journey at the end of the first week. As you know we had to pick up the train at Par and there were already passengers in it. We had to get seats in odd ones or twos & when there is a family it is very awkward on a long journey as they all require refreshments.

Our suggestion is - would it be possible to allocate a coach or coaches to accommodate the passengers boarding the train at Par?

Trusting this will receive your favourable consideration.

Yours faithfully, (Mrs) N.R. Boots

There is also a letter from 18 July from Mr R.W. Garlick of Station Road, Purton, requesting payment of 11s 6d taxi fare, which he had had to pay, 'owing to the non-running of the late train for returning TRIP passengers.' The letter is sent on by Mr F. Curtis, Station Master's Office at Purton, for the attention of W. Lampitt, Esq. District Commercial Superintendent, Gloucester. Mr Curtis points out that Mr Garlick is a Swindon Works employee, in the R. Shop, Loco., who had returned on the Special Train holding a free ticket and that a Special Train had been timetabled to depart Swindon at 11.03 p.m., 'as per noticed G.247 (Operating)'. On 4 August Mr Lampitt communicates with R.A. Smeddle, enclosing various correspondence in this respect. A handwritten note is added to this correspondence dated 6 August, stating, 'the position explained to Mr. Garlick, and accepted, we did not advertise a Special Train to Purton therefore his application is not in order'. This refers back to a memo dated Friday 19 June, in which it is stated that, 'certain additional trains between Swindon and Purton, Swindon and Wootton Bassett and Swindon and Highworth were agreed, with the exception of the late train to Purton on 11 July' (for which it was anticipated there would be only nine passengers). However, the matter is obviously still not completely settled as a further memo from Lampitt to Smeddle dated 10 August, encloses a copy of the notice No.G.247 and points the finger of blame elsewhere, 'I understand the Special Train arrangements on page three were made in conjunction with the Bristol District Operating Superintendent'. If we examine Page 3 of the identified document, one can see that there is indeed a train booked to leave Swindon at 11.03 p.m. and arrive in Purton at 11.12 p.m. Mr Garlick was clearly correct and he clearly deserved to be reimbursed his taxi fare.

REVIEW AND THANK YOU

TRIP was over and the Works was once again back to normal working. The challenge of TRIP 1953 had been met and, 'as far as can be ascertained', to quote Mr Smeddle, it had 'worked very smoothly'. Considering the large number of those who had travelled, and the small numbers of complaints or problems identified, one would have to agree with him. On Monday 6 July he wrote a standard letter of thanks to those staff who had helped make TRIP 1953 happen. Although standard in content, each letter was addressed personally, Dear Len, Dear Eric, Dear Jim, Dear Dennis, Dear John, Dear Roy, Dear Bruce, Dear Bert, Dear Aubrey, Dear Les, Dear Alan.

I wish to express my sincere thanks for your help and co-operation with the arrangements for the Swindon Works Annual Holiday 1953.

To J.J. Finlayson and H.G. Johnson, he wrote:

I wish to express my appreciation to the members of your Staff who assisted in this matter and particularly to those members of your office staff who assisted in compiling the necessary data regarding the numbers travelling and in the writing and distribution of the free tickets.

The employees side of the Works Committee also expressed their satisfaction of the arrangements and wished their appreciation to be conveyed to all those concerned in the operation.

This brief run through of 1953 gives us an insight into the depth and breadth of detail behind this gargantuan administrative operation, whilst also giving it a 'human' face.

~ CHAPTER SIX ~

THE END OF TRIP

The post-Second World War era brought huge changes – political, social and economic – to the people of Britain, all of which had a knock on effect for the railways and Swindon Works. Nationalisation meant that the Great Western Railway Co. ceased to exist. Swindon Works, whose 100th birthday had slipped by almost unnoticed during the war effort in 1943, was no longer the flagship of the GWR, but was now under the BTC, The British Transport Commission, along with all the other railway works in the country. The Mechanics' Institution also felt the effects of these winds of change, the most notable being the assumption of the administration of TRIP by the railway itself.

During the Second World War, holidays were taken as, when and if possible. TRIP, with its Works closure, was resumed in 1946 but with some notable changes. In 1947 a forty-four-hour week was gradually introduced, which meant no more work on Saturday mornings, making it easier still to get away for TRIP. The 1950s found the British public keen to have holidays and keen to travel, however, with the new found prosperity, people were beginning to find alternative means of transport. TRIP numbers never returned to the heady 20,000 plus, but remained impressive in terms of modern era numbers being 15,000 plus. The 1960s were times of swingeing cuts and redundancies on the railways and great changes in Swindon and the Works. The last steam locomotive to be built at the works was completed in March 1960. Engine No.92220, *Evening Star*, marked the end of an era. The numbers employed 'Inside' began to drop rapidly, 8,022 in December 1962 down to 5,104 by July 1967. By 1973, staff employed at the Works had fallen to 2,200.

TRIP, like the railways and Swindon Works itself, went through many changes in its lifetime, although the essence of it remained the same. The number of days of holiday went up and down until legislation in 1913, brought in to help the workers, forced them to lose several days holiday and to settle to one week. Later, immediately after the Second World War this became two weeks and Swindon Week became Swindon Fortnight, from Saturday to Saturday. It went from an unpaid lock-out to one week with basic pay, to two weeks with basic pay to, finally, two weeks with pay that included an agreed bonus. It started with a group of 500, grew to an amazing 29,000 and finally fell back down to just one Special Train. It was originally exclusive to members of the Mechanics Institution but eventually became available to all employees within Swindon Works. It went from being able to travel just anywhere on the Great Western Railway system, to then being able to travel on 'foreign metals', that is other companies' eg., the Southern, the LMS and LNWR, rail systems, to travelling to and across foreign countries. It was initially managed and administrated through the Mechanics Institution but was then taken over by the Staff Office.

TRIP Special Trains were part of the excitement of TRIP. Worked by GWR's wonderful engines, they could be anything up to fifteen coaches long. Sometimes they were too long for station platforms, such as at St Ives, and would have to be unloaded half at a time. (Swindon Museum & Art Gallery)

It was renamed Works Annual Holiday by officialdom, but the people of Swindon reclaimed it, and insisted on calling it TRIP. The one thing that remained constant through it all was that, to the employees in Swindon Works and to their families, travel on TRIP Special Trains was free.

The financial cost of TRIP in terms of the collective hours of administration throughout the year, the assembling, stabling, preparation and use of hundreds of coaches, the borrowing and running of large numbers of engines, the manpower dedicated to the working of TRIP traffic for the numerous outward and return journeys and the extra local trains run to link up with the Specials, the return and dispersal of empty sets of coaches after the journeys, the additional coaches required to strengthen regular trains to cope with additional TRIP passengers, must have been enormous. Surprisingly, even after Nationalisation, it did not have to attract revenue, it having been agreed as part of the 'rights' of Swindon Works' employees. As such, it was, as Richard Woodley says in his book *The Day of the Holiday Express*, something of a 'dinosaur'. An impressive dinosaur nevertheless, even in 1960. During the '60s between 12 and 15,000 were still departing on TRIP. Writing of the holiday traffic for 9 July 1960, which was the middle Saturday of TRIP fortnight, Richard says that the size of TRIP undertaking rivalled that other massive migration by rail, the Welsh Rugby supporters' annual pilgrimage to either Murrayfield or Twickenham. In February 1953 this had required thirty-one special trains, but it had fallen off over the years and had about twenty trains in 1960. This meant, to quote Richard, that 1960 TRIP was probably, 'the biggest single long-distance passenger movement on the WR'. What made it even more impressive than the Rugby migration was that, whereas the Rugby excursion was at a quiet time of the year in terms of train travel demand, TRIP was at its most demanding during the height of the summer season and it was still being run so as to not interfere with normal train timetable working.

Above: This must rank as one of the most atmospheric photographs taken of trippers and TRIP Trains. Swindon's indefatigable photographer, Mr Hooper, records this scene probably standing just to the west of Swindon West Signal Box adjacent to the barrow crossing which linked the main Carriage & Wagon Works, Drawing Office Stores and other parts of the Work with the main Carriage Works. From right to left: a 850 class 0-6-0 Saddle Tank, a 'Duke' class 4-4-0 being prepared to work one of the TRIP Trains, two dead engines awaiting works, the right-hand one of which is an 'Aberdare' class 2-6-0, and stood on the mainline a second 'Duke' class 4-4-0 on an up fitted goods train. The Works offices are prominent in the background and just to the right of the goods train the original Broad Gauge Engine Shed erected in 1846 can be glimpsed. Note the lovely gas lamp, the tall bracket signal and the general tidiness of the scene as well as the immaculate turn-out of the Trippers! (Brian Arman)

Opposite above: On Saturday 14 July 1956 one of the then three surviving Churchward's 'Star' class 4-6-0s, No.4056 *Princess Margaret*, heads returning TRIP Special No.40, the twelve-coach 5.40 p.m. from Paignton, through Aller Junction, approaching Newton Abbott at 6.07 p.m. No.4056 started work in July 1914 and was withdrawn from service in October 1957. (Peter Gray)

Opposite below: Returning TRIP Special was handled by 4-6-0 No.4909 *Blakesley Hall*, seen here as it skirts the Exe Estuary between Cockwood harbour and Starcross on 13 July 1957. The intended engine for this train had been modified 'Hall' class engine No.6995 *Benthall Hall*, which was seen leaving Newton Abbott for Paignton 'light engine' carrying the usual No.40 board. However, it must have been held-up from reaching Paington and to avoid further delay to the TRIP Special, No.40909, which had, apparently, been spare engine at Paington since 9.30 a.m. that day, was substituted – hence the chalked No.40 seen on top of the smokebox. (Peter Gray)

An iconic and much loved TRIP photograph that captures the romance and excitement, the traditions and the rituals, the magic and the myth of TRIP.

Swindon Loco was responsible for providing motive power for the TRIP Trains. As something of the order of twenty-five or more locomotives would be required, this would have been beyond the scope of the locally allocated available motive power, so engines were borrowed from near and far as well as utilising newly repaired locos from the workshops. This peaceful scene in around 1935 belies the hectic activity which TRIP preparation caused. This general view, although not taken during TRIP time, shows engines of Star, Hall, Saint and 43xx classes as well as a 51xx 2-6-2 tank and, on the right, the GWR's flagship engine 6000 *King George V*, some of which would have been used for TRIP work. (Brian Arman)

This is the 5.40 p.m. Paignton to Swindon TRIP Special. Heralding the new technology, the brand-new diesel-hydraulic 'Warship' class No.D823 *Hermes* is about to leave Newton Abbot at 6.13 p.m. on 9 July 1960. It displays the new system of four character numbers. The one indicates an Express Passenger train. The Z shows it is a Special. (Derek J. Frost)

Hewbert Cheesley worked in the boilershop and his son, Royston John Cheesley, seen here in the cab of a 'Warship' in the 1960s, perhaps getting it ready for TRIP duty, was an electrician on the diesel-hydraulics in the Works from 1956-1973. On being made redundant, Royston moved his family to Teignmouth, his favourite TRIP destination.

The excitement of TRIP still persisted through the 1960s. Now engines of the new era could be seen pulling TRIP Specials. One such in evidence on 9 July 1960 was the brand-new diesel hydraulic 'Warship' class No.D823, *Hermes*, which hauled the 5.40 p.m. return Special from Paignton. This had only been recently out-shopped from Swindon Works and so TRIP would have been one of its first long-distance mainline journeys. It would have been greeted with great interest by the Swindon Trippers, as the engines had always been part of the excitement of TRIP. The number of locomotives required to haul TRIP Specials greatly exceeded the number of suitable ones stabled locally. In its heyday, this could be anything up to thirty-two locomotives! In 1931 on Thursday 2 July and Friday 3 July, thirty-two engines were required. They were gathered from near and far. Seven came from Old Oak Common; two from Didcot. Two travelled from Wolverhampton; two from Neath; one each from Newton Abbott and Exeter; three came up from Cardiff and five from Bristol. The remaining nine were out of Swindon. One way of distinguishing TRIP Specials from other regular trains was by way of the train number. Up to 1959, regular trains had a three-digit number, but the Swindon Specials had only a one or a two-digit number. From mid-June 1960, the system changed to the four-character number as shown in the photograph of the Warship *Hermes*. Regular trains would have a letter A–V in the second place denoting destination area and steam engines only displayed the last 3 characters.

The locomotives that pulled the Specials had a special place in the hearts of Swindon people. Many would have been built in the Works. 'Stars', 'City', 'Saints', 'Bulldogs', 'Halls', 'County', 'Castles' – their names conjure up the romantic age of steam.

The 'Star' class was a TRIP stalwart that turned up for duty over many years. In 1912, the landmark year of night trains, 'Star' class, No.4011 *Knight of the Garter* hauled the 10.40 p.m. West Country Special, followed fifteen minutes later by the No.4015 *Knight of St. John*. Decades later in 1956, 'Stars' were still doing duty. No.4056 *Princess Margaret* pulled the return Special No.40 from Paignton. Also in 1912 the 'County' class carved its place into TRIP history with No.3832 *County of Wilts* and No.3824 *County of Somerset* featuring in an iconic photograph of TRIP day.

The 1970s saw a further reorganisation in Swindon Works and employee numbers were still going down. An early July edition of *The Evening Advertiser* in 1979 advises its readers that TRIP will begin in a week's time. It forlornly acknowledges that it is now 'a sad affair', although 'not entirely dead'. Although the Works rallied a little in the early 1980s, it was a slow, sad decline.

Despite a valiant fight and campaign, the Works closed on 26 March 1986. It was the end of an era. Swindon was no longer a railway town and there would never again be TRIP.

The Great Western Railway Co., Swindon Works and TRIP are a magnificent part of Swindon's rich railway heritage and culture. Whilst they are gone, they still live on in the memories of Swindonians, especially in the hearts of ex-Works railway families. It is fitting, therefore, that the last words should go to those who have lived and remember the dream.

GWR and Trip Fortnight

by Valerie Hillier

Our Dad worked in the railways
(On nights) his whole life through
And once a year at 'Trip' time
His holidays were due.

Out came the old brown suitcase
It was packed with all our things
Sometimes it was so crowded that
Dad tied it up with string.
Then early in the morning
Down to the sidings we would go
Meeting up with other families
Children's faces all aglow.

The trains would all be waiting
Steam coming from their stacks
We didn't go from the station
Just climbed up off the tracks.

Oh what excitement and such joy
For all us little girls and boys
We've waited for this all year
And now at last the day is here.

Mum always dressed us in our 'best'
And warned that it should not be messed
She packed a picnic for on the way
The journey seemed to take all day.

Some went off to Weymouth, Weston or Wales
Families to visit, or to stay in hotels
We went to Dawlish to stay with our Gran
Or now and then in a big caravan.

Mum and Dad had a deck chair each
While we sat in the sand or sea
And in the evening we went to the pub
My sister, my brother and me.

Building sandcastles and jumping waves
Cockling – winkling and crabbing
Mum hands out chips all covered in salt
Which our eager hands are grabbing.

After two weeks in the sun
Well, it never seemed to rain
It's time to pack the case once more
To go back home again.

We've all had such a wonderful time
And the journey home is quite sad,
But we know we will be back next year
Thanks to Great Western Railway and Dad.

The Last Train
Trip Morning, Swindon.
Departure of the 25,000

Sadly, the last TRIP Train was nowhere near as full as this. This, however, is how TRIP is remembered with trains full to bursting, the air full of excitement and everyone turned out in their best clothes determined to have a great time.

TRIP – ON THE TRAIN

by Mrs Margaret Suffolk (*née* Long)

It's June and mother's packing
A large trunk filled to the brim.
Our trunk was dark and solid
With a neat little wooden trim.

The trunk was sent in advance, you see,
In those days Dad didn't drive.
The trunk would be placed in the luggage hold
And be waiting for us to arrive.

For railworkers and their families
July brought 'Trip' again.
A week or two at the seaside,
Of course, we travelled by train.

Our home was full of excitement,
As we pulled on our cotton dresses.
Five little girls would form a queue
For mother to brush their tresses.

Then, off to Bradley's Corner
We would hurry to catch the bus.
Which would take us to Swindon Station
Where the train would be waiting for us.

A beautiful, large, steam engine,
With carriages to pull.
The families climbed on, then found a seat
Quite soon the train was full.

The flag was waved, the whistle blew
The sound from the tracks would clatter.
We're off, We''re off. We all would shout
Then we'd laugh and sing and chatter.

Sadly though those days are gone,
But our memories stay forever,
The Railway, 'Trip' and the great steam trains
Will we forget them? Never!

BIBLIOGRAPHY

BOOKS

Tim Bryan, *Return to Swindon*, Avon Anglia Publications, 1990
Trevor Cockbill, *When Summer Suns Were Glowing 1939 – 1941*, Quill Press
Trevor Cockbill, *The Finest Thing Out*, Quill Press, 1989
Ken Daniels, *Saundersfoot & Tenby*, Nonsuch Pub Ltd, 2006
Eric R. Moutford, *Swindon GWR Reminiscences*, Bradford Barton
O.S. Nock, *Tales of the Great Western Railway*
Alan S. Peck, *The Great Western at Swindon Works*, Oxford Publishing Co., 1983
A. Platt, *The Life and Times of Daniel Gooch*
J. Silto, *A Swindon History 1840 – 1902*, 1981
William Silto, *Of Stone and Steam: The Story of the Swindon Railway Village*, Barrucuda Books Ltd, 1989
Richard Tomkins & Peter Sheldon, *Swindon and the GWR*, Alan Sutton & Redbrick, 1990
Alfred Williams, *Life in a Railway Factory*. Duckworth & Co., 1915
Richard Woodley, *The Day of the Holiday Express: Western Region Services on 9 July 1960*, Ian Allan Publishing, 1996

ARTICLES

Clarice Baddeley, in *The Evening Advertiser*, 1986
Brian Cockbill, 'Memories of St. Ives by a Swindonian'
Mrs. Mabel Harding in *The Evening Advertiser*
Tom Richards, 'St Ives and The Swindon Connection'
John Turner, 'When the Specials Steamed into Weymouth'

JOURNALS/NEWSPAPERS

The Daily Chronicle
The Evening Advertiser
The Great Western Railway Magazine
The North Wilts Herald
The Railway Magazine
The Railway News
St. Ives Times
Southern Times
The Swindon Advertiser, The Evening Advertiser
The Tenby Times Annual 2006

SOURCES

STEAM Museum of the Great Western Railway Archives
Swindon Borough Council Reference Library
Swindon Museum and Art Gallery
Public Record Office
Private Collections

LIST OF ABBREVIATIONS

MPSO	Motive Power Superintendents Office
DWAH	District Works Annual holiday
C&WW	Carriage and Wagon Works
OSO	Operations Superintendent's Office
WBO	Works' Booking Office
CMEE	Chief Mechanical and Electrical Engineer

BRITISH RAILWAYS (Western Region)   **THREE**
SWINDON WORKS ANNUAL HOLIDAY, 1962

West of England Trains

SPECIAL TRAINS WILL RUN AS SHOWN BELOW:—

		Starting from the Station Down Line Platform Friday, July 6th		Rodbourne Lane Sidings Entrance, Park Lane Saturday, July 7th	
		Platform 1 Train No. 1	Platform 4 2	5	10
		P.M.	P.M.	A.M.	A.M.
SWINDON	dep.	10.00	10.55	6.00	7.42
Wootton Bassett	"	—	—	6.12	7.54
Taunton	arr.	—	—	—	9.38
Exeter	"	—	—	—	10.28
Dawlish Warren	"	—	—	—	10.49
Dawlish	"	—	—	—	10.54
Teignmouth	"	—	—	—	11.02
Newton Abbot	"	—	—	—	11.12
TORQUAY	"	—	—	—	11.32
PAIGNTON	"	—	—	9.50	—
Liskeard	arr.	—	4.50 a.m.	—	—
Bodmin Road	"	—	5.06	—	—
Lostwithiel	"	—	5.13	—	—
Par	"	—	5.23	—	—
St. Austell	"	—	5.36	—	—
Truro	"	3.47 a.m.	5.58	—	—
Truro	dep.	5.00	—	—	—
St. Agnes	arr.	5.20	—	—	—
Perranporth	"	5.36	—	—	—
NEWQUAY	"	6.12	—	—	—
Redruth	"	—	6.22	—	—
Gwinear Rd.	"	—	6.33	—	—
Hayle	"	—	6.40	—	—
St. Erth	"	—	6.46	—	—
Marazion	"	—	6.54	—	—
ST. IVES	"	4.55	—	—	—
PENZANCE	"	—	7.04	—	—

On Friday night, July 6th
Passengers for PERRANPORTH and NEWQUAY travel by Train No. 1 in NEWQUAY portion. (Rear of Train).

Passengers for LOOE travel by Train No. 2, change Liskeard proceeding at 5.55 a.m.
Passengers for WADEBRIDGE and PADSTOW travel by Train No. 2, change Bodmin Road, proceeding at 7.50 a.m.
Passengers for FALMOUTH travel by Train No. 2, change Truro, proceeding at 6.43 a.m.
Passengers for ST. AUSTELL, TRURO and PENZANCE must travel by Train No. 2.

On Saturday, July 7th, passengers for PAIGNTON travel by Train No. 5 only.
Passengers for GOODRINGTON SANDS, CHURSTON, BRIXHAM (change at Churston), KINGSWEAR and DARTMOUTH travel by Train No. 10 and proceed from Torquay by ordinary train at 12.19 p.m.
Passengers for Minehead Line travel by Train No. 10 and change at Taunton.
Passengers travel on Train No. 10 and change at EXETER for:—
EXMOUTH and proceed at 11.15 a.m. from Exeter St. David's.
BUDE and proceed at 12.02 p.m. from Exeter St. David's.
SEATON and proceed at 11.45 a.m. from Exeter St. David's.
BARNSTAPLE, ILFRACOMBE and BIDEFORD and proceed at 11.34 a.m. from Exeter St. David's.
Note.—The three rear coaches of Train No. 10 will be detached at Newton Abbot.
Passengers for PLYMOUTH, DEVONPORT and LAUNCESTON ONLY travel by the ordinary train from Swindon, Saturday morning, July 7th, due Plymouth N. Rd. 11.35 a.m.
Passengers for WESTON-SUPER-MARE travel by ordinary services.
On Sunday to Friday, July 8th to July 20th inclusive, passengers may travel on ordinary services.

RETURN ARRANGEMENTS.
Passengers must return as shown below; those from intermediate or branch line stations must connect with the train at the nearest point.

		Saturday July 14th		Saturday July 21st	
		Train No. 29	30	39	37
		P.M.	P.M.	P.M.	P.M.
PENZANCE	dep.	—	2.25	—	2.25
ST. IVES	"	—	1.56	—	1.56
Marazion	"	—	2.31	—	—
St. Erth	"	—	2.48	—	2.45
Hayle	"	—	—	—	2.50
Gwinear Rd.	"	—	—	—	3.01
Truro	"	—	3.33	—	3.33
St. Austell	"	—	3.58	—	3.58
NEWQUAY	"	—	2.30	—	2.30
St. Columb Rd.	"	—	—	—	—
Roche	"	—	—	—	—
Par	"	—	4.16	—	4.16
Bodmin Road	"	—	4.32	—	4.32
Liskeard	"	—	4.50	—	4.50
Plymouth N. Rd.	"	—	5.31	—	5.31
PAIGNTON	"	5.40	—	5.40	—
Torquay	"	5.50	—	5.50	—
Newton Abbot	"	6.10	—	6.10	—
Teignmouth	"	6.20	—	6.20	—
Dawlish	"	6.28	—	6.28	—
Dawlish Warren	"	6.35	—	6.35	—
Exeter	"	—	7.14	—	7.14
Taunton	"	—	8.05	—	8.05
SWINDON	arr.	9.40	10.03	9.40	10.03

On Saturdays, July 14th and 2 st—
Passengers from ST. IVES will depart 1.56 p.m. and travel on through coaches to Swindon.
Passengers from FALMOUTH depart 2.05 p.m. and join Specials No. 30 or 37 at Truro.
Passengers from NEWQUAY depart 2.30 p.m. and travel on through coaches to Swindon. PERRANPORTH passengers depart 1.55 p.m. and travel in Special from TRURO.
Passengers from PADSTOW depart 3.13 p.m. and WADEBRIDGE 3.24 p.m. connecting with Trains No. 30 and 37 at Bodmin Road.
Passengers from LOOE depart 3.50 p.m. connect with Trains No. 30 and 37 at Liskeard.
Passengers from DEVONPORT, PLYMOUTH and LAUNCESTON must travel on Special Trains shown above.
Passengers from KINGSBRIDGE depart 4.35 p.m. by ordinary train, change at Brent and join Specials at Newton Abbot.
Passengers from BUDE depart 3.09 p.m. (change Okehampton) and join Special at Exeter.
Passengers from SIDMOUTH depart 4.30 p.m. and from SEATON depart 4.27 p.m. Change at Exeter Central, joining Special Train at Exeter St. David's.
Passengers from EXMOUTH depart 5.15 p.m. change at Exeter Central, joining Special Train at Exeter St. David's.
Passengers from BIDEFORD depart 2.56 p.m. change at Barnstaple Jct., connect 3.50 p.m., arriving Taunton 5.48 p.m. and join Special.
Passengers from ILFRACOMBE and MORTEHOE travel on 2.55 p.m. ex Ilfracombe, arrive Taunton 5.48 p.m. and join Special.
Passengers from MINEHEAD depart 6.40 p.m. and connect with Special at Taunton.
Passengers from DARTMOUTH, KINGSWEAR, BRIXHAM, CHURSTON and GOODRINGTON SANDS travel by the 4.10 ordinary train ex Kingswear changing to Special Train at Paignton.
On any day, Sunday to Friday, passengers return by any ordinary services.

Chief Mech. and Elec. Engr's Dept.,
Swindon.   R. A. SMEDDLE
June, 1962.

PRINTED BY THE BOROUGH PRESS (SWINDON) LTD., EASTCOTT HILL, SWINDON

Whilst TRIP numbers are, by this time, decreasing, they are, as can be seen from this train's schedule, still significant enough to run four Specials to the West Country and four Special returns. Interestingly, the Sidings are still being used as a departure point.

Other titles published by Tempus

A History of the Steam Locomotive 'The Willing Servant'
DAVID ROSS

This is the first history of the world-wide development of the steam locomotive, from its earliest beginnings to its last days. It traces not only the history of design, construction and use, but the intriguing story of human involvement with the steam locomotive – of all inventions the one which seemed to possess a life and spirit of its own.

07524 2986 8

Sun, Sea and Sand The Great British Seaside Holiday
STEVEN BRIGGS AND DIANE HARRIS

This intriguing account is richly illustrated with a mixture of contemporary photographs and postcards, publicity material, posters and modern images. For those who remember the seaside holidays of their childhood this book will conjure up nostalgic memories, and for the modern historian it will be an invaluable chronicle of the inter-war period, when the annual holiday became part of the lives of large numbers of people for the first time.

07524 3964 2

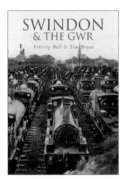

Swindon & the GWR
FELICITY BALL & TIM BRYAN

This book features rare and unpublished pictures of men and women who worked at Swindon, from the collection of images at STEAM: Museum of the Great Western Railway. Inluded in these pages are GWR locomotives, royal visits, staff outings and the famous TRIP holiday, showing a glimpse of life beyond the factory walls.

07524 2801 2

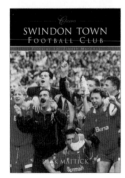

Swindon Town Football Club Fifty of the Finest Matches
RICHARD MATTICK

Since its creation as a result of the merging of two rival teams, St Marks and the Spartans, Swindon Town has been involved in thousands of matches and carried the name of Swindon all over the world. This book covers that historic period, as well as the many great League and cup matches played during the eighty years since Swindon became one of the founder members of the Third Division (South).

07524 2866 7

If you are interested in purchasing other books published by Tempus, or in case you have difficulty finding any Tempus books in your local bookshop, you can also place orders directly through our website

www.tempus-publishing.com